Discovery 2
Staying the Course

Bethany World Prayer Center
13855 Plank Road • Baker, Louisiana 70714
Phone: (225) 774-1700 • Fax: (225) 774-2335
Web site: www.bethany.com or www.bccn.com

STAYING *the* COURSE

Contents

Introduction

Congratulations on completing the first ten weeks of the Discovery classes! You have taken the time to build a firm foundation on Christ, the solid Rock, and you've learned how to strengthen your family. Your commitment to the Lord is growing daily, and your desire to be used in His kingdom is increasing. You are ready for the next step upward in your Christian journey. All you have to do is to *stay the course* that you've already begun and let God begin using you to reach out to others.

In this second level of the Discovery, you'll find out what serving God is all about. You'll be empowered and encouraged to see how God uses ordinary people like you and me to do extraordinary things for Him. It's going to be an exciting time as you discover an entirely new facet of your Christian faith.

This book, like the first book, is divided into two parts. In each of your class sessions, you will study one lesson from each part in the book. The first section of this book, "Charting Your Vision," will teach you how to have spiritual vision for souls and how to get actively involved in the process of sharing Christ through small group ministry.

Then, each week you will also study a lesson from the second part of the book. This section, "Conquering Your Land," will give you the tools you need to lay the spiritual groundwork for soul-winning and then will show you how to actually do it.

So, *stay the course* and get ready to discover the vision God has for *you!*

discovery

Charting Your Vision

STAYING *the* COURSE

2

God's Vision for the World

From the beginning of time, God has had an eternal vision for all humanity. His original plan was for all of us to live with Him in heaven in sweet communion and intimacy. That plan, as you know, was temporarily thwarted because of Adam and Eve's sin in the Garden. But God sent a Savior, His only Son, to redeem humanity and bring them back into fellowship with Him.

As you continue the Discovery, you are now ready to see the role that you can play in bringing others back to the Father. His vision will become your vision as you grow in faith and application of what you are learning. God will make you a soul-winner, and you'll become a partner with Him in bringing the Gospel to all the world.

There is nothing more rewarding than winning others to Christ, connecting them to the local church, training them in the ways of the Lord, and finally seeing them launch out to begin the cycle all over again. When you do that, God's vision has truly become your vision, and His heart has become yours.

So, get ready for this next exciting stage of knowing Christ. *Stay the course,* and continue your discovery of Him. You'll be glad you did!

Lesson 1
The Four Faces of the Vision: The Ox

Key Verse: *"Take My yoke upon you and learn from me, for I am gentle and humble in heart, and you will find rest for your souls. For my yoke is easy and my burden is light"* (Matt. 11:29–30 NIV).

Key Scriptures:
Ezekiel 1:4–10
John 13:14–17
Philippians 2:7
2 Timothy 4:5
Luke 10:18
Matthew 9:37
1 Corinthians 9:9, 19

Objective: The purpose of this lesson is to explain the four "faces," or values, of the vision and to explain how being a servant is the best way to bring others to Christ.

Introduction: In Ezekiel 1:4–10, the prophet Ezekiel had a stirring vision from God. This Old Testament saint saw four massive beings within a great cloud in the midst of a windstorm. Each creature had the form of a man, but each had four faces: the face of an ox, a man, an eagle, and a lion. These same creatures are also described in Ezekiel 10:14 and Revelation 4:6–8. For some reason, these four faces are important to God, and He wants them right near His throne.

These four faces represent four "faces" of God's vision for the world. Some scholars say they also represent the four Gospels. Regardless of their exact meaning, they are creatures of life and represent life in God in all its fullness. For that reason, we are going to examine each face in detail and what it means to you as you continue your discovery of God.

I.   What is the significance of the four faces?

A.   Israel used these same four faces.

1. According to Alfred Edersheim in *Bible History: Old Testament* (Logos Research Systems, Inc., Oak Harbor, 1997), Israel had these four faces on the banners that they marched behind in the wilderness.

   a. Four tribes led the way in the march. Judah (the lion) was first, and they had two other tribes with them. Then came Reuben (the man) and two other tribes. Third came Ephraim (the ox) with two more tribes, followed by Dan (the eagle) with the last two tribes.

   b. When all the tribes were camped together, an interesting formation occurred. It was quite a sight to behold: twelve tribes in the shape of a cross, with the three-tribe groups aligned in each direction.

2. From this, we can see a looking towards the cross and what it stands for. The cross of Christ is the central value of God's vision.

B.   The four faces represent the four _____ of the vision of God.

1. They are the faces (values) with which we Christians march into the world. We must have each of these values operative in our lives in order to be powerful, effective Christians.

2. As you discover your purpose and calling on your journey of faith, you'll find that everything begins with the first value: serving, or the "face of the ox."

II. What is the face of the ox?

A. The face of the ox represents _____ (John 13).

1. Jesus gave the best example of serving when He washed the feet of His disciples. No one in the group at the Last Supper wanted to assume this menial, dirty job of washing feet.

2. Christ took the basin and towel and carefully cleaned the dusty feet of the Twelve. He said, "Now that I, your Lord and Teacher, have washed your feet, you also should wash one another's feet. I have set you an example that you should do as I have done for you. I tell you the truth, no servant is greater than his master, nor is a messenger greater than the one who sent him. Now that you know these things, you will be blessed if you do them" (John 13:14–17 NIV).

3. Christ took upon Himself the form of a servant (Phil. 2:7). His heart was not proud. He said, "Take my yoke upon you and learn of me; for I am meek and lowly in heart" (Matt. 11:29 KJV).

B. _____ is the secret to multiplication.

1. Many animals become useful only after their wills are broken. Then they are no longer stubborn, rebellious, and independent. They become faithful, loyal, and humble.

2. An ox, for example, must be broken before it can serve under a yoke. It can plow only after it has learned to surrender its will to its owner.

3. Satan is arrogant and proud. He left heaven in rebellion (Luke 10:18). Lost people are called disobedient because their hard hearts keep them from obeying the Gospel (1 Pet. 2:7–8). They are not yet broken.

4. Brokenness comes from a revelation of the cross. Your will must bend and break in the same way Jesus surrendered His will at Gethsemane when He said, "Not as I will, but as You will" (Matt. 26:39b NKJV). Submission to God's authority is essential.

5. Christ broke the loaves before He multiplied them. He also said that "unless a grain of wheat falls into the ground and dies, it remains alone; but if it dies, it produces much grain" (John 12:24 NKJV). Brokenness and "death" always precede multiplication.

C.   The ox is a worker in the _____.

1. An ox is involved in all aspects of the harvest: the plowing, the reaping, and the threshing. One ox can produce an entire crop for the farmer. The ox represents the "work of an evangelist" (2 Tim. 4:5).

2. Jesus said, "The harvest is plentiful, but the workers are few" (Matt. 9:37 NIV). The ox represents the patient, diligent work of a soul-winner, a person who is praying, cultivating relationships, sowing spiritual seed, and reaping the harvest.

3.   In Discovery 2, you will learn how to be a fruitful soul-winner through prayer and witnessing. You will become a spiritual ox!

D.   _____ **is the secret to winning souls (1 Cor. 9:9, 19).**

1.   Paul referred to the ox's threshing of the wheat and thus having a right to the harvest (v. 9). He also said, "I have made myself a servant to all that I might win the more" (v. 19 NKJV).

2.   You will win people to the Lord when you serve them. Someone said, "People don't care how much you know until they know how much you care." When you serve them in practical ways, it opens their hearts to your message. This is called servant evangelism, and it is the face of the ox in action.

Summary: God has a big vision for the entire world! He longs for everyone to come to a saving knowledge of the truth and to spend eternity with Him in heaven. As Christians, we have the wonderful privilege of sharing God's vision with those who do not yet know Him.

God's vision has four "faces," or values, that help us understand it. The first value is serving others. When we embrace that value, we are like the hardworking, faithful ox that serves its master in the harvest. We allow God to "break" us, and we willingly get into the yoke of service to others. This is servant evangelism, and it is the best way of winning others to Christ.

Questions and Discussion Points

1.   What does the face of the ox represent, and why is the ox a good example of this trait?

2. Why must we be "broken" before we can be useful in God's kingdom? Have you ever experienced this breaking in your life? Are you willing to undergo continual breaking that you might be used of God?

3. Jesus' ministry largely consisted of service to others. List some ways that Jesus served. What can you learn from His example of serving?

4. Why do so few people want to serve? Are you willing to serve in any way? Are there limits to what you will do for God? Examine your heart in this area.

5. Do you know someone that you could reach out to through servant evangelism? What could you do for that person? Make plans to do it this week!

The Four Faces of the Vision: The Ox

Scripture Memory for Discovery 2, Week 1

"Take My yoke upon you and learn from me, for I am gentle and humble in heart, and you will find rest for your souls. For my yoke is easy and my burden is light" *(Matt. 11:29–30 NIV).*

Monday: Matthew 1:1–2:23 _____

_____

_____

Tuesday: Matthew 3:1–5:12 _____

_____

_____

Wednesday: Matthew 5:13–6:18 _____

_____

_____

Thursday: Matthew 6:19–8:4 _____

_____

_____

Friday: Matthew 8:5–9:26 _____

_____

_____

Saturday: Matthew 9:27–10:42 _____

_____

_____

Sunday: Matthew 11:1–12:21 _____

_____

_____

Special Prayer Requests _____

_____

_____

_____

_____

Lesson 2
The Four Faces of the Vision: The Man

Key Verse: *"Then He said to His disciples, 'The harvest is plentiful, but the workers are few. Therefore beseech the Lord of the harvest to send out workers into His harvest' "* (Matt. 9:37–38 NASB).

Key Scriptures:
Ephesians 4:11
Luke 10:33
Acts 9:1–30

Objective: The goal of this lesson is to teach the necessity of every believer to be connected to the body of Christ, the local church, through relationships. This lesson will stress the importance of developing solid and healthy relationships that help new believers grow in faith.

Introduction: Very few new believers remain in the church unless they form meaningful relationships with other Christian believers. Satan knows this and does all he can to break fellowship between believers and to get them to isolate themselves from one another. He knows that the accountability, comfort, and encouragement that come from close relationships in the body of Christ are a direct threat to him and the kingdom of darkness. Thus he works to sever bonds of relationship at every turn.

In Lesson 1, we studied "the face of the ox" and how that represents serving in the body of Christ. In this lesson, we are going to study "the face of the man" and how that represents pastoring new believers and connecting them to the local church.

I. What is the face of the man?

A. _____ is important in the body of Christ.

1. Satan knows that relationships provide protection. They bring accountability, comfort, and encouragement in times of difficulty. Satan, therefore, will stop at nothing to keep Christians from connecting to other Christians in close, meaningful relationships.

2. Our human nature craves smaller, more intimate relationships and is not satisfied with just being part of a large, anonymous crowd. Jesus knew this and formed a small group of twelve disciples that traveled with Him and worked alongside Him in His ministry. In our church, we follow this pattern and form relationships in small groups.

3. John Wesley, founder of the Methodist Church, placed each of his believers in a small group, or class, as he called it. Twelve people met each week and shared with the others in their class the temptations they had encountered the past week and how they had overcome them.

B. The face of the man represents the work of a _____.

1. A pastor is someone who looks after others, like a shepherd does with sheep. A pastor, like a shepherd, cares for his sheep's needs, checks their health, makes sure they are being fed, and protects them from danger.

2. In the church, some serve in the office of a pastor (Eph. 4:11), but there are many others who are pastoral workers. They assist the pastor in caring for the sheep. They

are trained by the pastor to help him care for the flock, much as a nurse helps a doctor to care for his patients.

3. Jesus said, "The harvest is so great, but the laborers are so few" (Matt. 9:38 NLT). He saw that people were like sheep without a shepherd (Matt. 9:36). We must ask God to give us the heart of a pastor for the sheep.

C.   The Good Samaritan was a "pastor of one" (Luke 10:33–35).

1. Pastoring starts with "one." Actually, to get one individual *out* of eternal hell and *in* to heaven is a major contribution to the kingdom of God! *One* soul is worth a lifetime of work. The Good Samaritan illustrates this principle beautifully.

2. The priest and Levite were too pious to touch someone who was half-dead. This beaten, abused man represents the millions of people who are unchurched, bound, and broken. They are the "underworld," those forgotten by the church.

3. The Samaritan poured his entire attention on "one." He healed him, bound his wounds, hospitalized him, and paid his bill. He even returned to check on him. This is the spirit seen in the face of the man.

II.   The story of Saul of Tarsus shows the importance of the face of the man (Acts 9:1–30).

A.   Saul had a miraculous conversion (v. 3).

1. Saul fell to the ground before a blinding light. He heard the voice of Christ and was converted to Christianity. His testimony of conversion from a murderer of Christians to an apostle to the Gentiles is one of the greatest proofs of the Gospel of all time.

2. In spite of his dramatic conversion, Paul still needed the face of a man. Millions are being converted around the world, but if they never see the face of a man (relationships), they will not last.

3. The Lord told Ananias, a disciple in Damascus, to go and meet with Saul (v. 11). Jesus even told him the exact address and name of the man he was to minister to. Ananias was the one chosen to present the first view of the face of a man to Saul.

B. Saul needed the face of a man (v. 17).

1. For three days, Saul was blind. He had time to think and reflect on his sinful life. Israel spent three days at Mount Sinai, and when we first come to Christ, we also need three days alone with God to let Him speak to us on the issues of our hearts. That's why we set aside three days for new believers to go on an Encounter Retreat.

2. Ananias laid hands on Saul, and Saul was healed of blindness. Literally, the first face he saw was the face of a man: Ananias. Similarly, every new convert needs a disciple to directly connect to, face-to-face.

3. Ananias also ministered water baptism and the baptism in the Holy Spirit to Saul (v. 17). He filled in the gaps in Saul's spiritual experience. The Encounter should be the place where we fill in the gaps in the lives of new believers.

C. Saul was _____ to the body of believers (vv. 19–22).

1. For a number of days after his encounter, Saul stayed with the disciples. He "kept increasing in strength" (v. 22 NASB) and grew bold in his witness for Christ. All new believers need other Christians to hang out with and from whom they can receive teaching, strengthening, and training.

2. This is the work of a "pastor of one." Saul of Tarsus became Paul, the greatest apostle of all time. Ananias had no idea that he would be working with the man who would become known as the apostle to the Gentiles. Multitudes of souls were saved and discipled through Paul, but none of it would have happened without Ananias's early ministry to him.

3. Christian leaders must work with every precious soul God gives them, just as though each has the potential of the apostle Paul. God is looking for faithful leaders who, like Ananias, will be willing to present the face of a man to those who have come to Christ.

Summary: We all need relationships in the body of Christ, especially new believers. Without genuine connection to loving, more mature Christians, most new believers will not remain within the local church body.

Think about your salvation experience. You probably had someone who reached out to you, visited you in your home, invited you to a small group meeting, took you on an Encounter Retreat, and encouraged you to continue your journey in Christ. As you are growing in Christ, you now have the opportunity to begin showing others the same love and concern that others showed you. When you begin reaching out in this way, you are showing others the face of a man and helping them connect to the body of Christ.

Questions and Discussion Points

1. Who helped you grow in Christ immediately following your salvation? What did that person do for you? How did it help you?

2. How do relationships help mature us in Christ? How are your relationships helping you to grow?

3. Discuss the term *a pastor of one.* Are you willing to let God use you in this way?

4. What role does the Encounter Retreat play in connecting believers to the body of Christ? How did your Encounter Retreat help you connect?

5. All ministry begins small. God will never entrust you with thousands if you will not be faithful to minister to even one. What are some ways you could start ministering to one other person? Ask God to give you "one," and start planting seeds into that person's life.

The Four Faces of the Vision: The Man

Scripture Memory for Discovery 2, Week 2

"Then He said to His disciples, 'The harvest is plentiful, but the workers are few. Therefore beseech the Lord of the harvest to send out workers into His harvest' " (Matt. 9:37–38 NASB).

Monday: Matthew 12:22–13:23 _____

_____

_____

Tuesday: Matthew 13:24–14:21 _____

_____

_____

Wednesday: Matthew 14:22–15:39 _____

_____

_____

Thursday: Matthew 16:1–17:27 _____

_____

_____

Friday: Matthew 18:1–19:15 _____

_____

_____

Saturday: Matthew 19:16–20:34 _____

_____

_____

Sunday: Matthew 21:1–22:14 _____

_____

_____

Special Prayer Requests _____

_____

_____

_____

_____

Lesson 3
The Four Faces of the Vision: The Eagle

Key Verse: *"We proclaim Him, admonishing every man and teaching every man with all wisdom, so that we may present every man complete in Christ"* (Col. 1:28 NASB).

Key Scriptures:
Deuteronomy 8:1; 32:10–11
Numbers 20:12
Acts 11:26
Hebrews 5:14
1 Corinthians 9:24–27
1 Timothy 4:7

Objective: This lesson will show how Christian maturity develops and how we can yield to its outworking in our lives.

Introduction: Every believer is called to maturity. Maturity, however, does not happen automatically all on its own. Just as excellence is the product of careful planning, Christian maturity is the product of discipline and effective mentoring. As we cooperate with the work of the Holy Spirit and with the guidance of more mature Christians in our lives, we will continue to grow spiritually. In fact, we will grow and mature to the point where we become spiritual eagles, flying high above every trial and circumstance of life.

I.   What is the face of the eagle?

A.   God trained Israel in the wilderness (Deut. 32:10–11).

1.   When Israel came out of Egypt, they were delivered from the power of Pharaoh (win). Then, they were brought to a three-day meeting with God at Mount Sinai (connect). Next, they were ready to learn the lessons of the wilderness (train).

2.   God used the symbol of the eagle to illustrate the learning process for His people. Eagles carefully and methodically train their young to fly, soar, and hunt. All the while, they watch over them, encircling, caring for, and guarding them as the apple of their eye.

3.   The eagle symbolizes the third face of the vision, and that represents training, moving a disciple into excellence in every area of life.

B.   The principle of _____ underlies all training.

1.   *Order precedes multiplication.* That little statement tells us why God sometimes takes so long to work in our lives. Anything that is out of order is usually unproductive (for example, a gas pump, a vending machine, an escalator, and so forth). Christians who never get their lives in order will never be productive and fruitful.

2.   Israel had to be put into order. God gave them banners, trumpets, the tabernacle, the priesthood, and a civil government. He even arranged their tribes in a military formation around the tabernacle. They went from being a nation of slaves to being a nation of sons.

3.   Even while you are in the Discovery classes, God is working in your life and character to put you into order: in your family, your finances, your health, your attitudes, your mind, your emotions, your relationships, and in many other areas.

C.   The eagle represents _____.

1.   Eagle Scout is the highest level someone can attain in scouting. It represents the successful accomplishment of a number of smaller tasks that lead to the ultimate recognition of Eagle Scout.

2.   Eagles have incredible vision, able to see small prey from great distances. They can dive at high speeds to catch fish they have seen from high altitudes. Storms do not threaten them, as they set their wings and allow the thermal winds to take them higher and higher.

3.   God wants to bring excellence into every area of your life. His discipline and order in your life will make you a better spouse, parent, businessperson, and leader. You may be in the "wilderness," but God has His eye upon you to train you in holiness.

D.   Paul had a clear method for developing leaders, or spiritual eagles (Col. 1:28 NKJV).

1.   Paul preached Christ (win), warned every man (connect), taught every man (train), and presented every man perfect (send).

2.   Paul and Barnabas demonstrated this method in Antioch: "For an entire year they met with the church and taught considerable numbers; and the disciples were first called

Christians in Antioch" (Acts 11:26 NASB). In the period of one year, Paul and Barnabas transformed converts into disciples.

3.   Our Journey and Discovery classes last about one year. In that amount of time, we hope to help an unbeliever become a believer, then a disciple, then a leader, and finally a servant.

II.   We can learn three main lessons from the eagle.

A.   First is the lesson of _____ (Deut. 8:1–5).

1.   God taught Israel how to follow simple structure in their daily lives. He used a cloud to direct their movement so they would learn how to follow the Holy Spirit's direction. He used manna to teach them how to obey simple instructions and be consistent every day.

2.   Our Discovery classes are meant to not only teach you, but also to train you. When God requires discipline and obedience, it means that He is dealing with you as a son (v. 5). Parents who do not care about their children's manners, attitudes, and work ethic are not really showing love to them.

3.   Training is the key to excellence. Paul said that our senses had to be trained so we could discern good from evil (Heb. 5:14 NKJV). He compared this training to the discipline needed to compete in a race or to attain physical fitness (1 Cor. 9:24–27; 1 Tim. 4:7–8).

4.   In this Discovery course, you are going to learn the spiritual discipline necessary to mature in Christ.

B. **Second is the lesson of _____ (Num. 11–14, 20).**

1. As soon as Israel left Mount Sinai, they began to complain against their spiritual authority. Their lustful eyes and flesh desired meat, something Moses had not given them. They grumbled against Moses, and as a result, many of them died from a plague (Num. 11:33).

2. Miriam and Aaron spoke against Moses because he had married a Midianite woman (Num. 12:1). God thus struck Miriam with leprosy until Moses prayed for her healing.

3. The ten spies who brought a rebellious, bad report lost their lives (Num. 13–14). The entire book of Numbers is about the forty years Israel had to spend in the wilderness in order to learn not to rebel against spiritual authority.

4. During the Discovery classes, you will learn the value of submission to spiritual authority. Of course, all those with spiritual authority must be humble and gentle, or God will judge them, like He did to Moses in Numbers 20:2.

C. **Third is the lesson of _____ (Num. 20:12).**

1. God said to Moses, "Because you have not believed Me, to treat Me as holy in the sight of the sons of Israel . . ." (NASB). The Lord is holy, and He must be honored by those who aspire to be leaders.

2. Nadab and Abihu (sons of Aaron, the high priest) were struck dead for offering "strange fire" (Lev. 10:1 KJV). God said to Moses, "By those who come near Me I must be

regarded as holy" (v. 3). Ananias and Sapphira learned this same lesson in Acts 5. God is holy, and He will not allow sin in His camp.

3.   During all three levels of Discovery, you will be growing closer and closer to the Lord. Learn the lessons of holiness, authority, and obedience in your walk and you will surely find yourself soaring like an eagle in the midst of a wicked world!

Summary: Spiritual eagles are mature disciples with lives of order and excellence. They have submitted to spiritual discipline and training, knowing its necessity in their lives. Because of their mature faith, they have learned to soar high above every trial and difficult circumstance that comes their way.

Mature leaders are obedient. Their wills are submitted to God's will, and they are quick to obey any instruction from the Lord. They also recognize spiritual authority and its place in their lives. They are committed to holiness, honoring and reverencing God. Because of their spiritual training and excellence, mature leaders "mount up with wings like eagles" (Isa. 40:31 NKJV). They do not grow weary in serving God and are full of strength and vitality. That is our call and that is our challenge: to be spiritual eagles, trained and ready to minister for the Lord.

Questions and Discussion Points

1.   Why is an eagle an apt symbol of Christian training? Which qualities of an eagle are most necessary to Christian maturity?

2.   Discuss the following statement: Order precedes multiplication. Then ask yourself the following questions: Is my life in divine order? Is my family life in order? Are there areas in which I need to improve? Am I ready for multiplication in my life and ministry?

3. As part of your spiritual training, God will teach you obedience. How has He done this in your life? What happened when you obeyed Him? What happened when you did not?

4. How does submitting to spiritual authority help you to grow in Christ? Are there limits to this submission? If so, what are they?

5. What is holiness? Is it a set of rules to follow? Is it subjective or objective? Give an example of how you have grown in holiness since beginning the Discovery classes.

The Four Faces of the Vision: The Eagle

Scripture Memory for Discovery 2, Week 3

"We proclaim Him, admonishing every man and teaching every man with all wisdom, so that we may present every man complete in Christ" (Col. 1:28 NASB).

Monday: Matthew 22:15–23:39 _____

_____

_____

Tuesday: Matthew 24:1–51 _____

_____

_____

Wednesday: Matthew 25:1–26:5 _____

_____

_____

Thursday: Matthew 26:6–56 _____

_____

_____

Friday: Matthew 26:57–27:31 _____

_____

_____

Saturday: Matthew 27:32–28:20 _____

_____

_____

Sunday: Mark 1:1–2:12 _____

_____

_____

Special Prayer Requests _____

_____

_____

_____

_____

Lesson 4
The Four Faces of the Vision: The Lion

Key Verse: *"Some Gadites joined David at the stronghold in the wilderness, mighty men of valor, men trained for battle, who could handle shield and spear, whose faces were like the faces of lions, and were as swift as gazelles on the mountain"* (1 Chron. 12:8 NKJV).

Key Scriptures:
Acts 4:31; 17:6
2 Timothy 1:7
Judges 6:5, 15
1 Samuel 17:35
Proverbs 28:1
1 Peter 5:8
Joshua 1:6–9; 3:5, 14–17; 6

Objective: In this lesson, we will explore the heart of the conqueror: what it is and how to possess it.

Introduction: God has called each and every one of us to live as more than a conqueror (Rom. 8:37). We are meant to live lives of victory, courage, and boldness because of our position in Christ. When we comprehend this truth, nothing can stop us from becoming forceful, courageous men and women of faith.

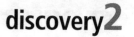

The lion has always represented power. Jesus Himself is called the Lion of Judah, describing His might and omnipotence as Lord of all. When we surrender our lives to Him, we can begin to draw upon that power and be transformed into mighty people of valor.

I. What is the face of the lion?

A. The lion is an animal of _____.

1. Our discovery of God's vision began with a study of the ox (serving) and continued with a study of the man (relationships) and a study of the eagle (training). Now we come to the ultimate intention of God's vision: conquest. We could say, therefore, that this vision we have been studying begins with *compassion* and ends with *conquest*.

2. Paul and Silas "turned the world upside down" (Acts 17:6 NKJV). They were not silent spectators in the Roman world. They were conquerors, men who shook nations and cities with the Gospel. These first missionaries were also mighty men of valor who had "the faces of lions."

3. Satan's most powerful weapon against Christians is fear and intimidation. Paul told Timothy, "God has not given us a spirit of fear, but of power, and of love and of a sound mind" (2 Tim. 1:7 NKJV). God must deliver us from all fear so that we can conquer the "Goliaths" in our lives.

B. The Old Testament reveals numerous examples of men who were like lions in their faith.

1. **Joshua:** After the forty years of training in the wilderness, Israel was poised to conquer the land of Canaan. Joshua took his people through the Jordan and conquered thirty-one kings en route to a powerful occupation of the Promised Land.

2. **Gideon:** From a silent, frightened farmer, Gideon became a valiant warrior. He led three hundred men into battle against an army too large to count (Judg. 6:5). His victory is an example of how one of the weakest and the least (v. 15) became an awesome deliverer of his people.

3. **David:** As a teenager, he killed a lion and a bear (1 Sam. 17:35). Then he fearlessly took on the challenge of Goliath, the 9-foot giant of the Philistines. With no fear, he ran toward the mammoth man and killed him with one stone.

C.   You need _____ in your life!

1. Proverbs 28:1 NIV says, "The righteous are as bold as a lion." When you know that you are righteous, made clean and pure by the blood of Jesus, you will have no fear of Satan's condemnation. This sense of confidence in your righteousness before God is the beginning of boldness.

2. The early church was "all filled with the Holy Spirit, and they spoke the word of God with boldness" (Acts 4:31 NKJV). Boldness comes from receiving the power of the Spirit. Timidity, fear, condemnation, and double-mindedness must all leave when you are filled with the Holy Spirit.

D.   "Lions" are dreamers and _____.

1.   Dreams, desire, and drive are the elements of the lion. Joshua dreamed of the Promised Land after first seeing it as one of the twelve spies. For forty years, his desire grew. Finally, his drive culminated in taking Israel across the Jordan and conquering the enemy's territory.

2.   The "lion" describes a heart that is fearless, bold, and powerfully moving forward to conquer. Satan knows that if you achieve this kind of spirit, you are a grave threat to him. He goes about like a "roaring lion" (1 Pet. 5:8), and only believers who are "lion-like" in the Spirit are a threat to him.

II.   There are four steps to spiritual conquest.

A.   _____ is the first step (Josh. 1:6–9).

1.   In this passage, Joshua had become the new leader of Israel. Moses had died, and now Joshua had to step up and lead. Everyone feels a sense of inadequacy when facing a new assignment. *Can I do it? Will people follow me? Am I prepared for the challenge?* These and other such questions run through our minds.

2.   Courage is not the absence of fear, but the will to do what is right. For Joshua, the time was right and his destiny lay before him. All he had to do was to step courageously into his divine purpose.

3.   Similarly, as you stand before your "Jordan River," you are going to have to exercise courage in order to step up to conquest.

B.   _____ is the next step to conquest (Josh. 3:5).

1.   Conquering the devil requires stepping up to another level of holiness and consecration. Joshua told the officers to consecrate themselves. This meant they had to disconnect from the world, fear, and the past. This is also what you have to do as you prepare yourself for major battle with the enemy.

2.   God instructed Joshua to have the priests carry the ark into the Jordan. This placed God's holiness in the very front of the battle. Satan fears your commitment to purity, holiness, and consecration. He trembles when you bring it into battle.

3.   Israel even had to circumcise all their children because they had not obeyed the Lord in the covenant (Josh. 5:2–7). Perhaps there are little areas of compromise and disobedience in your life that God is dealing with in order to bring you into conquest.

C.   **_____ comes next in the steps to conquest (Josh. 3:14–17).**

1.   The priests carried the ark of the covenant into the Jordan River. This was the point of no return. The moment their feet touched the water, however, the river dried up. God is waiting for you to make a commitment where there is no going back to safety.

2.   After crossing the river, Joshua chose twelve men to gather twelve stones from the Jordan riverbed and pile them on the shore of the Promised Land (Josh. 4:2). This represents the power of a team of twelve to conquer any fortress and spiritual stronghold the enemy is holding.

3.   God is going to put you on a team of twelve for spiritual conquest. You and the other eleven members will have great success working together to accomplish spiritual objectives in freeing many people from Satan's grip.

D. _____ **finally comes after taking the first three steps (Josh. 6).**

1. Jericho was "tightly shut up" (v. 1 NIV). Satan is holding thousands of people in his grip of death, but God has a strategy of pulling down those walls. We call this strategy "spiritual warfare." It uses God's weapons of praise, worship, and prayer to batter down the enemy's gates.

2. During Discovery 2, you will begin to pray the prayer of three. You and two other people will "circle the walls of Jericho" every day for thirty days as you pray for the lost. Satan's grip will be removed, the blinders will come off their eyes, and they will come into the kingdom of God.

3. Prayer, fasting, and worship were the strategies Jesus used in spiritual conquest. With over five billion lost people on the planet, we need to get started! Are you ready to cross over to the other side of _your_ Jordan?

Summary: The face of the lion in Ezekiel's vision (Ezek. 10:14) represents conquest. Christians are victors, both in this world and in the world to come. But we will never walk in the fullness of victory until we begin identifying with the lion and acting upon the boldness that the Holy Spirit gives.

To be a spiritual conqueror takes courage, consecration, and commitment. Courage propels us forward in the battle even when our hearts are afraid. Consecration keeps us from compromise and disobedience that would hinder our ability to conquer. Commitment causes us to walk into the deep waters of faith, sure of God's ability to bring us to the other side.

The "face of the ox" makes us servants. The "face of the man" bonds us to others in the body of Christ in healthy, life-affirming relationships. The "face of the eagle" teaches us to soar to new realms in the Spirit as we submit ourselves to training. But the fourth face of the vision, the "face of the lion," represents our coming to maturity in Christ as a fearless, courageous, victorious child of God.

Questions and Discussion Points

1. Fear is one of the most crippling emotions in a person's life. What are some fears you have had, and how did they hinder your spiritual walk? Has God delivered you from some of your fears? How did He do it? Do you still have areas of fear in which you need a touch from the Lord?

2. Discuss this statement: Courage is not the absence of fear. How would you define courage? Who is the most courageous person you have ever known?

3. Discuss how consecration is an attitude of the heart rather than a list of dos and don'ts.

4. What role does commitment play in facing a spiritual challenge?

5. Share your greatest spiritual victory. What did you learn from the experience?

6. In what area are you currently facing a spiritual battle? In what ways could you fight more effectively? Share your struggle with one other person and let him pray with you.

The Four Faces of the Vision: The Lion

Scripture Memory for Discovery 2, Week 4

"Some Gadites joined David at the stronghold in the wilderness, mighty men of valor, men trained for battle, who could handle shield and spear, whose faces were like the faces of lions, and were as swift as gazelles on the mountain" (1 Chron. 12:8 NKJV).

Monday: Mark 2:13–3:35 _____

_____

_____

Tuesday: Mark 4:1–5:20 _____

_____

_____

Wednesday: Mark 5:21–6:29 _____

_____

_____

Thursday: Mark 6:30–7:23 _____

_____

_____

Friday: Mark 7:24–9:1 _____

_____

_____

Saturday: Mark 9:2–50 _____

_____

_____

Sunday: Mark 10:1–52 _____

_____

_____

Special Prayer Requests _____

_____

_____

_____

_____

Lesson 5
The Creative Power of Vision

Key Verse: *"The Lord said to Abram, after Lot had separated from him, 'Now lift up your eyes and look from the place where you are, northward and southward and eastward and westward; for all the land which you see, I will give it to you and to your descendants forever' "* (Gen. 13:14–15 NASB).

Key Scriptures:
Genesis 14:14, 20; 15:6, 12
Romans 4:3, 17–21
Hebrews 11:6

Objective: This lesson will teach the student the creative power of vision and why it is necessary in his ministry for the Lord.

Introduction: Vision is an essential ingredient in Christian life and ministry. Proverbs 29:18 KJV says, "Where there is no vision, the people perish." Life without vision is drudgery and boring routine; life with Spirit-inspired vision is productive and fulfilling.

After Abram separated from Lot, God gave him a vision of His divine plan. Abram saw the vastness of the land that God wanted to give before he ever possessed any of it. The creative power of that vision propelled Abram forward and kept his faith strong, even during times of severe testing, as he waited for its fulfillment.

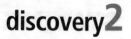

When God gives us a vision of something, we see it in its completed form. We see what will be before it ever comes into existence. The power of this vision motivates us to wait in faith for its fulfillment.

I.   God gave Abram a great vision (Gen. 13:14–17).

II.   This vision had five major parts to it.

A.   _____: **Separate from Lot.**

   1.   Lot represents worldly, carnal believers. Their interests are centered on money, pleasure, and riches. Lot "lifted up his eyes" (Gen. 13:10 KJV) and set his mind and vision on the things of the earth.

   2.   God reserves His vision for those who will choose a higher path: the path of commitment, service, and love for Him. Lot's vision was short-range, but Abram's vision was long-range.

   3.   The walk of a powerful leader can be lonely because he has chosen to focus on the eternal rather than the temporary. You will never see the vision of souls and cells while in the companionship of those who are like Lot. If you surround yourself with carnal believers who have no concern for the eternal, you will lose the vision.

B.   _____: **"Walk through the land" (Gen. 13:17 KJV).**

1. Having vision is the first step, but walking it out is the second. You must encompass your vision. Abram walked around the entire land of Israel, claiming his vision. Joshua walked around Jericho, claiming his vision.

2. A walk-through is a simulated vision. For example, actors do a walk-through of a play to get the feel of what it will be like on opening night. For a spiritual vision to come to pass, the leader must first walk through the vision, carefully preparing for it in his mind.

3. You should walk through your vision for souls and cells. Let God give you the vision for your growth this year, and then carefully rehearse it in your mind and spirit until it is as though you have already been there.

4. Seeing the vision is important, but walking it through is what makes the vision as real as if it had already taken place.

C. _____: "**He armed his trained servants**" (Gen. 14:14 KJV).

1. The third step to fulfilling your vision is training. The Hebrew word for *train* in this verse means "to narrow," "to discipline," "to dedicate," and "to initiate." Your dedication to being trained and seeing others trained will determine your future and long-term success. It is true that without a vision the people perish, but it is also true that without people the vision perishes.

2. Each person in a cell or a church is unique. Each has certain levels to which he can attain, but all can run the race. That includes you and those you will eventually mentor. Thus your third focus is to become more than an average bill-paying, kid-raising, grass-mowing believer who shows up at cell meeting. Your goal is to become a confident, competent soul-winner and discipler of others.

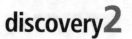
3.   We are not into birthing cells, but we are into discipling people. When you begin discipling others, love them, because one day they will be your assistants in carrying out the vision God has given you.

D.   _____**: "He gave him tithes of all" (Gen. 14:20 KJV).**

1.   The fourth principle of fulfilling your vision is to become a giver to others. Abram shared God's blessings with Melchizedek, who understood that the more he gave, the more he would multiply.

2.   A stingy, grasping spirit can never multiply. A fear of sharing your blessings stunts your growth. Before you can move to the next level of your vision, God always requires you to give.

3.   Find someone needier than you and sow a seed into his life. God will take that seed and multiply it back to you for your vision to come to pass.

E.   _____**: "He believed in the Lord" (Gen. 15:6 KJV).**

1.   Faith is essential for a vision to come to pass. Abram saw the vision and became fully persuaded of it (Rom. 4:3, 17–21). "Without faith it is impossible to please Him" (Heb. 11:6), and God will always test your faith in the vision.

2.   Abram passed through a "horror of great darkness" (Gen. 15:12 KJV). Satan will seek to intimidate you, harass you, and steal your vision from you. You must persevere in faith, even through the darkest, loneliest times. The battle is always hottest before the breakthrough!

3.   A leader who has separated himself from worldly vision, walked through the vision in his heart, trained others to help him in the vision, given to others who are also in the vision, and stood in faithfulness waiting for the vision will surely see it come to pass!

Summary: The creative power of vision will transform believers from church attendees to powerful leaders. The vision for leadership, however, comes in stages. First, we separate from the world and carnal pleasures. Second, we meditate and rehearse the vision in our minds and hearts. Third, we receive necessary training. Fourth, we plant seeds that God can multiply towards the fulfillment of the vision. Fifth, we stand in faith, waiting on God to bring the vision to pass.

Questions and Discussion Points

1.   When you have a vision, what must you first see?

2.   How is Lot like the carnal-minded believer?

3.   Explain the different aspects of the vision that Abraham possessed.

4.   Do you have a vision for your life and ministry? If so, what is it? If not, begin asking God to give you vision.

The Creative Power of Vision

Scripture Memory for Discovery 2, Week 5

"The Lord said to Abram, after Lot had separated from him, 'Now lift up your eyes and look from the place where you are, northward and southward and eastward and westward; for all the land which you see, I will give it to you and to your descendants forever' " (Gen. 13:14–15 NASB).

Monday: Mark 11:1–12:17 _____

_____

_____

Tuesday: Mark 12:18–13:31 _____

_____

_____

Wednesday: Mark 13:32–14:52 _____

_____

_____

Thursday: Mark 14:53–15:32 _____

_____

_____

Friday: Mark 15:33–Luke 1:25 _____

_____

_____

Saturday: Luke 1:26–80 _____

_____

_____

Sunday: Luke 2:1–52 _____

_____

_____

Special Prayer Requests _____

_____

_____

_____

_____

Lesson 6
The Biblical Basis of Cells

Key Verse: *"How I kept back nothing that was helpful, but proclaimed it to you, and taught you publicly and from house to house"* (Acts 20:20 NKJV).

Key Scriptures:
Matthew 9:35–38; 10:1–7
Acts 2:46; 5:42; 10:30, 44–48; 12:12; 16:15, 31–34, 40
Romans 16:5
1 Corinthians 16:19
Colossians 4:15
Philemon 1:2

Objective: The goal of this session is to demonstrate the biblical principles that apply to meeting in homes.

Introduction: The New Testament church was not established by constructing a building, but by forging a community of believers that met both in large gatherings and in houses. This New Testament pattern is still the best way to "do church."

Most churches have no problem with the public meeting of its members. In fact, weekly Sunday morning meetings and Wednesday midweek services are the norm for most traditional churches. However, a growing

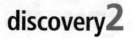
number of churches are realizing the need for smaller, more intimate home meetings in addition to the weekly services. These home meetings are called by various names, one of which is cell meetings.

I. The New Testament records the example of small groups that meet in homes.

A. Jesus established this pattern.

1. Jesus often held meetings in homes and ministered in homes (Matt. 9:10, 23, 28; Mark 1:29–31; 2:15).

2. Jesus instructed His disciples to win a city by first finding a home in which to minister (Matt. 10:11–15; Luke 10:1–7).

B. The early _____ followed this pattern.

1. There were two types of ministry in the early church.

   a. They met daily at the temple (Acts 2:46; 3:1–3; 5:21, 25, 42).

   b. They met from house to house (Acts 2:41–47; 5:42; Rom. 16:5; 1 Cor. 16:19; Col. 4:15; Philem. 1:2).

2. The Gospel often spread through entire households.

a.   The household of Cornelius received the Gospel (Acts 10:30–33, 44–48).

b.   So did Lydia's household (Acts 16:14–15).

c.   The Philippian jailer's household also received the Gospel (Acts 16:31–34).

II.   There are ten specific advantages of the cell strategy.

A.   First is the development of _____.

1.   The church should not be centered upon a single person doing all the work. With the cell strategy, leaders are prepared for the task of the ministry (Eph. 4:12).

2.   In cell ministry, each believer—man or woman, youth or adult, professional or nonprofessional—has the opportunity to develop his entire spiritual potential.

B.   Effective _____ results from the cell strategy (Num. 11:10–30).

1.   Cells care for the needs of the brethren.

2.   Cells ensure that people get the advice and counsel they need.

3.   Cells help people get answers to the questions they have.

4.   Cells show people how to apply truth to their lives.

5.   Cells motivate believers in the ministry.

C.   With the cell strategy in place, the church _____.

1.   The church is transformed when it begins to multiply its vision in the lives of its members.

2.   The difference between a program-based church and a cell-based church is like the difference between fishing with a fishing pole versus fishing with a cast net.

3.   The cell model provides the "net" for a great catch of souls (see John 21:6–8).

D.   The cell strategy effectively closes the "back door" of the church.

1.   With cells, the "bus effect" is eliminated.   The comparison is to a bus that is always filled with the same number of people, but with a makeup that keeps changing because people pass through as passengers for only a short time.

2.   With the cell strategy, we not only keep believers within the church, but we also form them into leaders. This we do on a continual basis.

E.   The cell strategy _____ the church.

1.   In a bonfire, the flames keep burning because the fire keeps feeding them fuel. Similarly, the cell structure helps us to stimulate one another to love and good works (Heb. 10:24).

2.   It is difficult for people to remain separated from the Lord and the vision if they are closely connected to a cell. When used in the correct way, the cell strategy creates relationships as strong as a cord of three strands (Eccles. 4:9–12).

F.   The cell strategy creates a church without walls.

1.   With the cell strategy, the potential for growth does not depend upon the size of the building, because the vision does not depend upon four walls. Cell vision and multiplication turn the focus outside the church, rather than keeping it inside only (Matt. 9:35–38).

2.   If we lose the outward perspective, we lose the goal of the church here on the earth (John 4:34–38).

G.   The cell strategy facilitates ministry.

1.   We develop our ministry skills through practice. In cells, we get the opportunity to teach, pray, serve, sing, practice hospitality, and engage in many other practical demonstrations of ministry.

2.   First we see, and then we do. In the cells, we have mentors to set examples for us. From them, we learn how to minister to others.

3.   This makes it possible for us to become the leaders that God calls us to become (Eph. 2:10).

H.   The cell strategy reveals spiritual _____.

1.   After we are born again, we begin to discover the gifts that God has given us to help advance His kingdom.

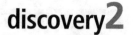

2.	Cell groups give us the opportunity to serve, and in that serving, we discover the gifts that God has placed within our lives (Rom. 12:1–3 NKJV).

3.	Once we discover our gifts, we have a better understanding of how God wants to use us in the body of Christ.

**I.	The cell strategy promotes _____ rather than _____.**

1.	The cell church is not based upon getting volunteers to run programs so that the church can function. Rather, it is based on relationships formed within the cell groups.

2.	The early church was established in both community and relationships (Acts 2:44–47).

**J.	The cell strategy fosters _____.**

1.	We are all called to give an account of our lives before God (Rom. 14:12).

2.	We must also be accountable to one another (Eph. 5:21).

3.	We must give an account to those who have oversight for our lives (Heb. 13:7, 17).

4.	We are called to help, love, exhort, encourage, and minister to one another. In other words, we are accountable for one another (Rom. 12:10; 14:13, 19; 15:7, 14; Gal. 5:13; 6:2).

Summary: The early church met both publicly in the temple and in smaller group settings in the home. This biblical pattern is still a valid pattern for us to follow in our churches. Public gatherings give believers the sense of belonging to something greater than themselves and enable pastors to preach and minister corporately to their flocks. Public gatherings release the power of concerted prayer and celebrate the bond of Christian community.

As important as public worship is, there is another aspect that is just as vital. That is ministry in small group settings. The early church met from house to house, and we, too, need small, intimate settings where we can form relationships with others in the church. The small group (cell) structure can minister to individual needs in a way that is not possible in once-a-week corporate settings. Cell groups ensure that believers are cared for, loved, and helped to grow in Christ. The relationships formed in cell groups are life-affirming, enduring, and motivating.

Nothing can take the place of biblical ministry in small groups. That is where the real life of the church takes place, and that is where leadership is developed.

Questions and Discussion Points

1. Why do you need to be part of a small group as well as part of the larger church body?

2. How do cell groups provide for effective pastoring of their members? How has your cell group "pastored" you? What kinds of things have you learned by being a part of your cell group?

3. What opportunities for ministry do you have in a cell group? Are you taking advantage of the opportunities you have in your group?

4.   The core value of cell ministry is the development of close, personal relationships. What kinds of things could you do to help foster closer relationships in your cell group?

5.   How do cell groups keep people accountable? How much influence should your cell group have in your life? Discuss.

The Biblical Basis of Cells

Scripture Memory for Discovery 2, Week 6

"How I kept back nothing that was helpful, but proclaimed it to you, and taught you publicly and from house to house" (Acts 20:20 NKJV).

Monday: Luke 3:1–4:13 _____

_____

_____

Tuesday: Luke 4:14–5:26 _____

_____

_____

Wednesday: Luke 5:27–6:42 _____

_____

_____

Thursday: Luke 6:43–7:50 _____

_____

_____

Friday: Luke 8:1–56 _____

_____

_____

Saturday: Luke 9:1–56 _____

_____

_____

Sunday: Luke 9:57–10:42 _____

_____

_____

Special Prayer Requests _____

_____

_____

_____

_____

Lesson 7
Seven Secrets of a Multiplying Cell Group

Key Verse: *"Then God blessed them, and God said to them, 'Be fruitful and multiply; fill the earth and subdue it; have dominion over the fish of the sea, over the birds of the air, and over every living thing that moves on the earth' "* (Gen. 1:28 NKJV).

Key Scriptures:
Genesis 1:2–24; 49:4
John 17:12
Galatians 4:19
Colossians 4:12
Mark 11:13

Objective: This lesson will glean from the story of creation seven secrets of growth and multiplication of a cell.

Introduction: God is an abundant God, and He wants His children to walk in abundance. Everything He does is full of life, power, blessing, and greatness. He does not do things on a small scale!

As we become leaders in the body of Christ, God wants to bless our cell groups with growth, multiplication, and abundance. He is not satisfied—and neither should we be—with "business as usual" week after week in our cell groups. With His help, we can lead groups that are full of vitality and that reflect the abundance of God.

I.   Genesis 1 establishes the principle of growth and multiplication.

A.   God's environment teems with _____.

1.   When God created the heavens and the earth, He carefully orchestrated seven stages that brought prolific multiplication. If all seven of these things are present in a cell group, that group will accomplish the vision of multiplication.

2.   The Discovery classes are a school for raising up leaders. The goal of Discovery is not just the acquisition of more knowledge, but learning how to use that knowledge to advance the kingdom of Jesus Christ. We advance that kingdom through cell groups that expand, release, and multiply.

B.   "_____" is the key to the vision.

1.   "Pastoring" is a good word for connection in the vision. It means to watch, warn, and war for those sheep for which we are responsible. Every aspect of the principle of twelve vision is all about pastoring people and connecting them to the body of Christ.

2.   Jesus said, "While I was with them, I was keeping them in Your name which You have given Me; and I guarded them and not one of them perished but the son of perdition, so that the Scripture would be fulfilled" (John 17:12 NASB). It takes time and effort to check on, encourage, defend, warn, and nurture sheep. But that's the example that Jesus set for us, and that's what we need to do.

3. Pastoring is the real work of the vision. Sheep cannot guide themselves, feed themselves, or protect themselves. They need shepherds to do that for them. When we become shepherds over part of God's flock, we begin reaping fruit for the kingdom of God.

II. There are seven components of a multiplying cell group.

A. _____ (intercession) is the first component (Gen. 1:2).

1. The Holy Spirit brooded over the chaos of the unformed earth in order to bring life. There is no substitute for the role that intercession and spiritual warfare play in a multiplying cell group. If the leader is not a prayer warrior and does not train others to pray, there will never be lasting fruit.

2. Paul said, "My children, with whom I am again in labor until Christ is formed in you" (Gal. 4:19 NASB). Obviously, Paul interceded and travailed in prayer for those he was responsible for. They were like children to him, and he loved them deeply.

3. Epaphras, one of Paul's disciples, was also an intercessor for souls. This is what Paul said about him: "Epaphras, who is one of your numbers, a bondslave of Jesus Christ, sends you his greetings, *always laboring earnestly for you* in his prayers, that you may stand perfect and fully assured in all the will of God" (Col. 4:12 NASB, emphasis added).

4. When your cell group is just beginning, there are many ways you can intercede for God's work of multiplication to be accomplished. Praying over pictures of lost friends and relatives or praying over pictures of stadiums full of people can help you focus your prayers on the harvest. You can also pray over follow-up cards, and you can use

the prayer of three to begin praying for your cell. You can pray Scriptures about the harvest and do spiritual warfare based upon Scripture. You might decide to fast one day a week, take prayer walks or drives, and spend half nights of prayer in the prayer center to launch your cell group's mission of multiplication.

B. _____ **is the second component (v. 5).**

1. As a cell begins with three people, these members must come into a covenant of holiness, transparency, and commitment to the vision. Worldly distractions, unfaithfulness, hidden sin, and hidden agendas must all be dealt with as the cell comes into covenant agreement. "Darkness" must be replaced with "light," just like when God created light out of the darkness.

2. The cell leader might want to take the other two members with him to attend an Encounter in order to minister together during the small group sessions. They must commit to developing their relationships with one another through utilizing text messages, e-mails, phone calls, and visits. They should share meals, fellowship, and ministry. The cell must become a family to its members, and an element of teamwork and trust must be established. As someone once said, "Loosely knit cells produce loose Christians."

C. Solidarity is the third component (v. 9).

1. Water is unstable and fluid; land is solid and substantial. The next element the cell must have is a solid footing, like the dove sought when released from Noah's ark. The cell should not be like Reuben, the firstborn of Jacob, who was called "unstable as water" (Gen. 49:4 KJV).

2.   The cell must establish itself in a routine of time, place, and agenda. The cell should not move around, constantly changing its time and place of meeting. The meeting should hold to the one-hour format to enable people to come without committing an entire evening. These are the ways "dry land" is established in our cells.

D.   Seed is the next component (v. 11).

1.   The first three elements of multiplying cells deal with the spirituality, sanctification, and solidarity of the cell. Once these three elements are in place, the cell is ready to produce fruit.

2.   Christ rebuked a fig tree for having leaves, but no fruit (Mark 11:13). In other words, it looked good, but real substance was missing.

3.   Each of the three cell members must learn how to engage in personal evangelism, connecting others to the body of Christ, bringing people to Encounters, and pastoring those they bring to the cell. In this way, they are planting spiritual seeds that will reap a harvest.

4.   Unfruitful members will stop the vision. The leader must pray over and intercede for his cell members until they are able to produce fruit.

E.   _____ is the fifth component (v. 14).

1.   God established the sun, moon, and stars to mark the seasons, days, and years. In this way, the schedule of the universe was set. In the cell, "seasons," "days," and "years" represent the three parts of the divine "clock" that keep the cell running smoothly.

2. "Days" represents a daily schedule of devotions. Cell members should use the same Bible reading plan so that they can converse about their daily *rhema* words. Consistency in daily devotions is critical to the ongoing fruitfulness of each member.

3. "Seasons" represents a quarter of a year, or three months. Each "season," the cell should establish its goals for that quarter. The cell should set goals for network meeting attendance, Journey enrollment and participation, and enrollment and continuance in the Discovery classes.

4. "Years" represents a cell's annual goals. The cell should have an annual goal of birthing three new cells.

F.   "Swarms" (multitudes) are the sixth component (v. 20 NLT).

1. "Seed" plus "schedule" produces "swarms"! Now the cell begins to teem with new life, new faces, new experiences, new goals, new victories, and new leaders. The covenant of the original three members has now produced a cell full of people who come for weekly pastoring.

2. A crowd draws a crowd. Growing from three to six can take months, but growing from six to twelve may take only weeks! The better the original three pastor and connect others to the group, the faster the group will grow, because they will retain everything they birth.

G.   _____ is the final component of multiplying cell groups (v. 24).

1.   At this point, the cell is now quite large, and the leader can begin to select those leaders in the cell that are "after his kind." Each cell takes on the particular flavor and emphasis of the leader as he selects those he can best work with for an extended period of time.

2.   The DNA of the cell takes shape based on where most of its fruit has come from: businessmen, athletes, single mothers, students, or any other type of group. All the team focuses on reaching that kind of person.

Summary: All cells have the potential for growth and multiplication within them, but not all cells will tap into the power that is theirs for the asking. Healthy, multiplying cells have prayer as the underlying basis of all they do. They are committed to holiness and lives of integrity. They are dedicated to the vision of winning souls and making disciples, and the members work together to achieve that goal.

Multiplying cells emphasize evangelism and pastoring those they win to the Lord. They have a consistent plan for individual growth as well as growth as a cell. As the cell increases in size and maturity, it begins taking on its own unique flavor and moving forward in its purpose. Members from the cell begin opening their own cells, and so the process is duplicated.

Questions and Discussion Points

1.   What is the key to the vision? Explain how this key played an important role in your growth in Christ.

2.   How important is prayer to the birth and growth of a cell? What is the prayer focus of the cell that you are currently attending?

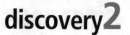

3.   Explain how a schedule helps a cell to grow and multiply.

4.   What is meant by the word *solidarity,* and why is it so important to the growth and multiplication of a cell?

Seven Secrets of a Multiplying Cell Group

Scripture Memory for Discovery 2, Week 7

"Then God blessed them, and God said to them, 'Be fruitful and multiply; fill the earth and subdue it; have dominion over the fish of the sea, over the birds of the air, and over every living thing that moves on the earth' " (Gen. 1:28 NKJV).

Monday: Luke 11:1–54 _____

_____

_____

Tuesday: Luke 12:1–53 _____

_____

_____

Wednesday: Luke 12:54–14:14 _____

_____

_____

Thursday: Luke 14:15–15:32 _____

_____

_____

Friday: Luke 16:1–17:19 _____

_____

_____

Saturday: Luke 17:20–18:34 _____

_____

_____

Sunday: Luke 18:35–19:44 _____

_____

_____

Special Prayer Requests _____

_____

_____

_____

_____

Lesson 8
The Power of a Small Breakthrough

Key Verse: *"Then Jonathan said to the young man who bore his armor, 'Come, let us go over to the garrison of these uncircumcised; it may be that the Lord will work for us. For nothing restrains the Lord from saving by many or by few' "* (1 Sam. 14:6 NKJV).

Key Scriptures:
1 Samuel 14:6–16
Zechariah 4:6

Objective: In this lesson, we will explore the dynamics of a spiritual breakthrough and how to set spiritual goals that can be attained.

Introduction: There is power in a small breakthrough! In Matthew 10, Jesus sent out the Twelve to minister to the multitudes. He gave them goals and showed them how to accomplish them. He knew that success in their initial steps of ministry would generate further success in ministry.

When we are able to achieve a seemingly small goal, it spurs us on to greater achievement. Faith is all about moving from stage to stage in our relationship with the Lord. We take small steps of faith, which in turn lead to bigger steps of faith. Never downplay the power of a small breakthrough. It has the potential of revolutionizing your entire ministry for God.

I. **God can bring victory through something seemingly small (1 Sam. 14:6–16).**

    A. **There is power in a small breakthrough.**

        1. Jonathan and his armor-bearer demonstrated a principle that has proven effective in both the military and the corporate world: the power of a small breakthrough.

        2. When Jonathan and his armor-bearer defeated twenty men on half an acre of land, the rest of the army simply melted away in all directions (v. 16).

    B. **"Then panic struck the whole army" (v. 15 NIV).**

        1. Although only twenty men had been defeated, the rest of the army panicked, and the "little" victory led to an even greater one.

        2. We often look for a huge change of strategy to turn a situation around, but a small breakthrough can actually bring the momentum to effect big changes over time.

II. **A sense of _____ must exist before you can experience a breakthrough.**

    A. **The vast power of a group's potential is tapped into when there is a sense of urgency and crisis.**

1. People have done amazing things when they knew they had a deadline to meet or their jobs were on the line if they didn't produce certain results.

2. Without that sense of urgency, most people will just float along in life, not ever really rising to the challenge of being all they can be.

B.   Cells will suffer if they lose their sense of urgency.

1. When a cell group loses its sense of urgency, meeting or not meeting is of no consequence.

2. The cell becomes stagnant, and the goals become distant.

3. Time passes with no results in the vision, and the leader becomes disillusioned or negative.

C.   The leader's task is to establish _____ within the group that bring a sense of urgency.

1. In our Scripture text, we see how Jonathan took it upon himself to do something out of the ordinary. By his action, he demonstrated to everyone else what could be done if they had courage.

2. In the same way, the cell leader will set the tone in his group as to what the members are expecting to see happen in the group.

III. The breakthrough strategy: Win a small victory in thirty days.

A. _____ the condition of your cell group.

1. Look at the status quo of your group: attendance, absences, visitors, souls saved, follow-ups, prayer, community outreaches, and other such things.

2. Do a good, hard inventory of your group in each area and identify the areas in which you need improvement.

B. Set an attainable goal.

1. Next, isolate one area and set a realistic goal for improvement over the course of thirty days.

2. Let the group help you come up with the goal and be a part of pursuing it in prayer and faith.

3. Don't try to totally transform your group overnight, but work on one area and change the results in that one area.

C. _____ your success.

1. Finally, evaluate your success at the end of the thirty days. The group will be excited about its accomplishment and the momentum gained.

2.   Reaching a crisis goal is likely to result in permanent change.

D.   Cell attendance could be an example of how to do this.

1.   If you have 10 people on your cell roster, perhaps only 5 attend on a weekly basis. Set as a goal for the cell to increase attendance by 20 percent (7 people attending) this month.

2.   You could accomplish this by having the members visit each person who comes sporadically or has dropped out of the cell. A personal visit may uncover needs in their lives that they had not been willing to share with the group.

3.   When you reach your goal, the small breakthrough will achieve permanent results in your group. The meetings will be stronger, and the group will be motivated by accomplishing the goal.

IV.   Here's how to have twelve months of consecutive small victories.

A.   For each month, set a goal in one specific area.

1.   When Jonathan defeated twenty soldiers in a half acre, the multitude began to run in terror.

2.   The devil loves to try to convince us that we can never change or improve our cells, but that is just not the case!

B. **Remember: The victory will come through the** _____ _____ _____
_____.

    1.   Zerubbabel was faced with a seeming impossibility in rebuilding the temple of the Lord. Zechariah prophesied to him and encouraged him, saying, " 'Not by might nor by power, but by My Spirit,' says the Lord of hosts" (Zech. 4:6 NKJV).

    2.   He reminded Zerubbabel, "Who has despised the day of small things?" (v. 10).

    3.   Another example comes from the life of Nehemiah. Nehemiah's people were very discouraged over the impossibility of rebuilding the wall. Nehemiah, however, set them in place to build one small section of the wall apiece; thus, the entire expanse of wall was eventually completed.

C. **Be encouraged!**

    1.   God will give you small victory after small victory as you implement the strategy of the small breakthrough.

    2.   You will find your group winning souls, connecting new converts, raising up leaders, impacting the community, sending out prayer teams, and birthing new cells in the unreached areas of your city and in the world.

Summary: Big victories and great accomplishments begin with small steps. This is true in the spiritual world as well as in the natural world. The power that is unleashed in small beginnings generates a momentum that effects an outcome greater than the individual steps taken.

We can use this truth in our cell groups to see them become dynamic places of ministry. We don't have to settle for "business as usual," but we can release our faith to see God give us the breakthroughs we need in our groups. So start today, start small, and start believing God to unleash the power of a small breakthrough!

Questions and Discussion Points

1. Summarize what prompted Jonathan to take the action he took in 1 Samuel 14:6–16. How does this apply to the cell leader who may be struggling?

2. Explain how to win a small breakthrough in thirty days.

3. According to Zechariah 4:6, what is the most important thing to remember about attaining a small breakthrough?

4. Set a goal for your cell or the one you are a part of. Follow the steps outlined in this lesson and keep track of what happens in the next thirty days.

The Power of a Small Breakthrough

Scripture Memory for Discovery 2, Week 8

"Then Jonathan said to the young man who bore his armor, 'Come, let us go over to the garrison of these uncircumcised; it may be that the Lord will work for us. For nothing restrains the Lord from saving by many or by few' " (1 Sam. 14:6 NKJV).

Monday: Luke 19:45–21:4 _____

_____

_____

Tuesday: Luke 21:5–22:6 _____

_____

_____

Wednesday: Luke 22:7–62 _____

_____

_____

Thursday: Luke 22:63–23:43 _____

_____

_____

Friday: Luke 23: 44–24:50 _____

_____

_____

Saturday: John 1:1–51 _____

_____

_____

Sunday: John 2:1–3:36 _____

_____

_____

Special Prayer Requests _____

_____

_____

_____

_____

_____

Lesson 9
Entering Into the Vision

Key Verse: *"And it shall come to pass in the last days, says God, that I will pour out of My Spirit on all flesh; your sons and your daughters shall prophesy, your young men shall see visions, your old men shall dream dreams"* (Acts 2:17 NKJV).

Key Scriptures:
Luke 19:10
1 John 3:8
John 14:12; 17:18; 20:21
Joshua 1:1–9
2 Corinthians 5:14–16
Hebrews 11:6

Objective: The student will understand and embrace the vision of God to win souls for His kingdom.

Introduction: God has always had a vision for redeeming humanity back to Himself. He sent His Son to the earth to see that this vision came to pass. When we become born again, this vision of restoration birthed in the heart of God becomes our vision. We become an integral part of His plan for winning the lost, but if we fail to walk in the divine vision, we fail to fulfill His plan for our lives.

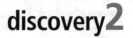

I. You must understand God's vision for your life.

A. You are called to fulfill the _____ of Jesus Christ.

1. The Word of God teaches that the mission of Christ Jesus was twofold: to seek and save that which is lost (Luke 19:10) and to destroy the works of the devil (1 John 3:8).

2. Jesus said that you are to do the same works that He did (John 14:12). Just as the Father sent Him, so He sends you into the world (John 17:18; 20:21).

3. Therefore, you have the same life mission that Jesus had: to seek and save that which is lost and to destroy the works of the devil.

B. You are called to _____ so that you might fulfill Christ's mission.

1. God's purpose in choosing you is so that your life might be productive for Him (John 15:16). He brought you into relationship with His Son so that you would manifest in your life the same features of fruitfulness that Jesus showed in His life (John 15:5–8).

2. As you fully appreciate your standing in Christ Jesus, you will be able to live free from the world (Rom. 7:4) and will start bringing forth the fruits of righteousness, love, and power.

3. There are five areas of fruitfulness that you should be demonstrating in your life as a disciple.

    a.   You should be growing in your development of the fruit of the Holy Spirit (Gal. 5:22–23). More and more, these qualities should be evident in your life.

    b.   Your mind should become more and more like Christ's as you train it to dwell on right thoughts and give access to the Holy Spirit's transforming power (Phil. 4:8–10; Rom. 8:5–8; Eph. 4:22–24).

    c.   Your deeds should bring honor to God and reflect a commitment to a life of service to God and His people (Col. 1:10).

    d.   You should be using and developing whatever spiritual gifts you have been given (1 Pet. 4:10; Rom. 12:4–6).

    e.   You should be fruitful in multiplying disciples (Acts 6:7).

C.   **You are called to support the "_____ of the house."**

1.   The term *vision of the house* refers to the specific vision that God has given the senior pastor of a particular local church. As a member of that local church body, you are to support the vision that God has given your pastor.

2.   You are called to fellowship and community within the church and its vision (Acts 2:46–47).

3.   You are called to walk in unity in the vision (Eph. 4:1–7).

4.   You are called to walk in one accord with others, having the same mind (Phil. 2:2). In this way, there will be no discord in fulfilling the vision.

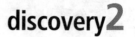

5. You are part of one body that is called to minister in unity under the anointing of Christ (Ps. 133:1–3).

II. There are three main "enemies" that will keep you from entering into the vision.

A. First is the enemy of _____ and _____ (Josh. 1:8–9).

1. God has not given you the spirit of fear and intimidation. That is very clear from Scripture: "For God has not given us a spirit of fear, but of power and of love and of a sound mind" (2 Tim. 1:7 NKJV). If you find yourself fearful about being able to enter into the vision, know that that thought is not from God. It comes from the devil, who would love nothing more than to keep you from being fruitful in the kingdom of God.

2. The enemy will also try to use discouragement to stop you from obtaining what God has promised. However, if you keep your focus on the fact that God is with you regardless of any circumstance you face, you can persevere.

B. Second is the enemy of _____ (Josh. 1:1–9).

1. God commanded Joshua to arise and take possession of the land. Joshua had to put feet to his faith before he could see God's promise come to pass.

2. If you are passive in your faith, you will never experience all that God has for you. You must assert yourself and act on what God has commanded you to do. Faith without corresponding action is really no faith at all (James 2:26).

C. **Third is the enemy of** _____ **(Rom. 8:6–7 NKJV).**

    1.   A carnal mind is one that is set on things that are worldly. The cares and pleasures of this world are more enticing to the person with a carnal mind than are the things of God.

    2.   You must set both your heart and mind on things "above," not on things "beneath" (Col. 3:1–3). In that way, you will guard yourself against carnal thinking and actions subtly infiltrating your life.

III. The vision has a divine, heavenly source.

A. **The vision originates from the Father (John 3:16; 20:21).**

    1.   The original vision to redeem the lost came from the very heart of God. He is the one who formulated and initiated the divine plan of sending His Son Jesus on behalf of the sins of all humankind.

    2.   His vision is your vision, and just as He sent Jesus into the world, so, too, does Jesus send you into the world. The vision to win the lost is not a manmade idea; it comes from the Father-heart of God.

B. **The vision grows and develops as you spend time in the** _____ _____ _____ **(Josh. 1:8; Ps. 1:1–3; Rom. 10:17).**

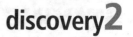
1.   The more you meditate on the Word of God, the more He reveals to you how to walk in a lifestyle of fruitfulness. The Word of God will inspire, correct, and challenge you. You will never be fruitful without its preeminence in your life.

2.   The Word of God will cause you to be successful in carrying out God's design for your life. It will teach you right standards of conduct and keep your walk with God pure. It will keep you humble before Him and aware of your total dependence on Him.

C.   The vision is imparted by the _____ _____ (Acts 16:6–9; 26:19).

1.   Paul acted according to the revelation of vision that the Holy Spirit gave. His own plans were set aside when the Holy Spirit revealed different plans. This is what you must do, too. No idea that you can come up with is better than the Holy Spirit's idea. Ask Him to give you His plan and vision, and then yield to it.

2.   Paul was careful to obey the vision as given by the Holy Spirit. He embraced it and then fulfilled it. When you first embrace the vision in your heart and then begin moving in obedience to it, you soon find yourself actually fulfilling it!

IV.   You must actually enter into the vision!

A.   Enter into the vision through the _____ (Luke 9:23; 2 Cor. 5:14–16).

1.   The cross is the crux of the Christian message and God's vision for the lost. At the cross, Jesus paid the ultimate price for sin when He willingly gave Himself as a sacrifice. The love that compelled Him to such action becomes yours as you embrace the cross and its message.

2.   As a disciple, you are challenged to pick up your cross and follow Jesus. As you live daily in the shadow of the cross, surrendering your own plans to His, you will come to see God's vision for the lost. His vision will become your vision, and His heart will be your heart.

B.   Enter into the vision through _____ (Matt. 6:6; 9:37–38).

1.   Prayer is two-way communication with God. What God has to say to you is always more important than what you have to say to Him! As you spend time alone with Him, He will begin speaking His vision to your heart. Listen for it, and seek it in prayer until it becomes a reality to you.

2.   Jesus knew the importance of prayer and thus directed His disciples to pray for workers in the harvest. Unless you are willing to be one of the workers in the harvest field, you will never receive the vision. Ask the Lord to send laborers into the harvest, and be willing to be one of them!

C.   Enter into the vision through _____ (Mark 1:17; Luke 5:27; Heb. 11:6).

1.   Jesus issued the call to follow Him to specific men He wanted to use in His work. Each one, however, had to make a personal decision to respond. Those who left all and followed Him were transformed into vessels for the Lord's service.

2.   Faith and obedience go hand in hand. If you trust God, you will obey Him. Your obedience is simply a reflection of the faith that is already within you. Grow in faith and obedience to God, and you will grow in His vision.

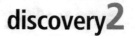
D.   Enter into the vision through _____ (Phil. 2:1–2).

1.   When you walk in unity and fellowship with others, you will accomplish greater things for God than you could ever accomplish alone. Your effectiveness is multiplied many times over. You need others, and they need you, too.

2.   By walking in unity, you walk in the fellowship of the Holy Spirit. The Holy Spirit will bring you into a life of fruitfulness and anointing.

Summary: What a glorious vision God has given us! There is no greater honor than being allowed to be a part of His vision to redeem lost souls. Jesus, of course, paid the price that made redemption possible, but we have a part to play in the process of winning the lost to Him.

We must first embrace the vision within our hearts and then move in faith and obedience to walking out the vision on a daily basis. We cannot afford to get distracted with worldly pursuits or to be crippled with fear and discouragement. We are called to be active, bold participants in the divine plan of redemption.

Questions and Discussion Points

1.   What is the vision of God, and how does it relate to you and your life?

2.   In which five areas does a person need to be fruitful? In which area are you strongest? Weakest?

3.   Discuss how passivity hinders fruitfulness in the vision. What excuses do people sometimes give for not doing the things that God has commanded them to do? Why are these not valid?

4. Why is the cross so central to God's vision of winning souls and making disciples? Have you had a personal revelation of the cross? If so, how has it affected you?

5. Discuss the relationship between faith and obedience. Why can you not have one without the other?

Entering Into the Vision

Scripture Memory for Discovery 2, Week 9

"And it shall come to pass in the last days, says God, that I will pour out of My Spirit on all flesh; your sons and your daughters shall prophesy, your young men shall see visions, your old men shall dream dreams" (Acts 2:17 NKJV).

Monday: John 4:1–54 _____

_____

_____

Tuesday: John 5:1–47 _____

_____

_____

Wednesday: John 6:1–59 _____

_____

_____

Thursday: John 6:60–7:44 _____

_____

_____

Friday: John 7:45–8:47 _____

_____

_____

Saturday: John 8:48–9:41 _____

_____

_____

Sunday: John 10:1–11:16 _____

_____

_____

Special Prayer Requests _____

_____

_____

_____

_____

Lesson 10
The Law of Brokenness and Service

Key Verse: *"The Lord is near to those who have a broken heart, and saves such as have a contrite spirit"* (Ps. 34:18 NKJV).

Key Scriptures:
1 Corinthians 1:27–29
James 4:10
Galatians 2:20
2 Corinthians 12:9–10
Mark 9:33–35; 10:35–45
John 12:24–26; 13:1–17
Philippians 2:5–11

Objective: This lesson will show the value of brokenness and how it leads to effective service in the body of Christ.

Introduction: Most people who are even halfway serious about their Christian walk express a desire to be used by God in His kingdom. Although they are aware of how much needs to change within them before they can experience God's power at work through them, they hesitate to really allowing God free rein.

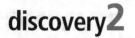

God, however, can work in us only if we come to a place of true brokenness before Him. Without that, we will continue to be led and influenced by self-will, self-centered desires, and self-knowledge. Only through brokenness can we truly learn total dependence upon God, and only by losing our lives for His sake will we find true fulfillment.

I. Brokenness occupies a very important place in the kingdom of God.

A. A humble, contrite heart is pleasing to God (Isa. 57:15; Ps. 51:17).

1. Isaiah 57:15 tells us that the same God who inhabits the heavens also seeks to dwell in the heart that is humble and contrite before Him. This attitude of humility and dependence upon God is known as brokenness.

2. According to Psalm 51:17, God never despises true humility and contrition. Contrition means living in a state of repentance and dependence upon God's grace. A humble, contrite heart rejects pride and self-promotion, because it acknowledges its deep, deep need of God.

B. Simplicity of spirit makes for _____ in God's kingdom (Matt. 18:1–4).

1. At the heart of your being should be a simplicity born of God in terms of trust and single-mindedness in following Him. This means becoming childlike in your trust and obedience to the Lord. Only in this way will you be able to walk in humility before Him and thus enable Him to use you for His divine purposes.

2. In most ancient cultures, age increased social status and authority. Children, therefore, were the most powerless members of society. It was different, however, in Jewish culture. Children were loved, not despised, by their parents; nevertheless, they had no status apart from that love and no power or privileges apart from what they received as total dependents on their parents (C.S. Keener and InterVarsity Press, *The IVP Bible Background Commentary: New Testament,* InterVarsity Press, Downers Grove, Illinois, 1993). As children of God, we are beneficiaries of His love and privileges.

3. W.W. Wiersbe has very appropriately remarked, "True humility is not thinking meanly of oneself; it is simply not thinking of oneself at all" (*The Bible Exposition Commentary,* "An Exposition of the New Testament Comprising the Entire 'BE' Series," Jkt. Victor Books, Wheaton, Illinois, 1989, 1996).

C. Brokenness leads to experiencing the Spirit without _____ (Phil. 2:5–11; John 3:34).

1. For Jesus, being "nothing" was a way of life. Long before He went to the cross, brokenness characterized everything He did. Although He was King of Kings and Lord of Lords, He willingly surrendered His rights and made Himself nothing.

2. Surrender and brokenness are the secret to walking in the fullness of God's Spirit. Jesus had no hindrances within Him, so God could pour the Spirit upon Him without measure (John 3:34).

3. The Father is just as willing to give you the Spirit without measure, but the limitations of your own heart will determine the measure of the Holy Spirit you actually experience.

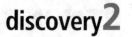
4.   In Jesus, God the Father had full access to pour in the Spirit without measure. In our lives, however, we are so often filled with emotional, intellectual, and spiritual clutter. Only brokenness can remove the clutter and make room for the Spirit.

D.   Brokenness releases a sweet "_____" (John 12:1–8).

1.   Before Mary could anoint the feet of Jesus, the alabaster jar had to be broken. Only then was the ointment available for use.

2.   In a similar way, you must be broken before the ointment of the Holy Spirit can flow out from you. Unless you are willing to be broken and become "nothing," God can never use you.

E.   Brokenness prevents Satan from gaining a toehold in your life (John 14:30; 17:14).

1.   The reason that Satan could never defeat Jesus was that there was nothing in Jesus but the Spirit of God. That meant there was no point whatsoever in which Satan could hold Jesus captive.

2.   The devil wants you to indulge your old nature and be led by it. In this way, he can reach into your life and gain entrance, since nothing good resides within your natural, carnal nature (Rom. 7:18). Brokenness, however, forces you to look to God in a new, deeper way that does not permit casual playing around with the devil.

F.   Brokenness is the mark of someone who has met with God (Gen. 32:22–32).

1. Jacob's struggle cost him everything he was and everything he had, that is, his name and his strength. However, in God's eyes, the night of Jacob's wrestling with the angel was the defining moment of his entire life. On that night, Jacob met God face to face and yet lived to tell the tale. He was never the same, though, because he bore the mark of God in his body.

2. The new Jacob (Israel) now walked with a permanent limp, but this seeming weakness was actually his greatest strength. When you meet with God, you are touched by His power and overwhelmed by His holiness. You, too, are marked for life.

3. To know that God has examined your life and in His love spared you from what you deserve—that is true brokenness. Brokenness like that is not weakness. It is the very source of strength in your spirit. After such an encounter with God, things will never be the same again. There will be an emptiness—not nothingness or meaninglessness—that only God can fill.

II. Having a _____ heart is also very important in the kingdom of God.

A. A servant is one who is not his own master but rather serves another.

1. If you want to know whose servant you are, look at what occupies most of your time, has priority in your heart, or takes most of your money. That is what you serve.

2. A servant of God is one who has dethroned himself and his interests and enthroned Jesus as Lord of all his life. In other words, he puts Jesus first, before anything else.

3. As a disciple of Jesus, you are expected to serve God only (1 Cor. 4:1). This means that you put God's kingdom first (Matt. 6:33) and do not serve riches, power, possessions, or anything else (Matt. 6:24).

B. A servant of the Lord has certain easily recognizable traits.

1. **He seeks first the kingdom of God (Matt. 6:33).** Nothing else is as important to Him as serving in God's kingdom.

2. **He is servant of all (Matt. 20:26–28).** Greatness in the kingdom of God comes from a life of service to others. The servant of the Lord does not look for others to serve him, but looks to see how he can serve others.

3. **He looks to his _____ for his reward (Matt. 25:21).** The servant of the Lord is not swayed by the opinions of others and does not need their approval. He works to please His Master, knowing that his reward comes from God.

4. **He serves others and in doing so serves the Lord Jesus (Matt. 25:31–40).** Nothing is too menial or lowly for the servant of the Lord, because he knows that service to others is service to Christ.

5. **He is willing to _____ himself, take up his cross daily, and follow the Master (Luke 9:23).** His life is one of surrender, sacrifice, and daily obedience to the will of God.

6. **He follows the example of Jesus in selfless acts of service (Luke 22:27).** His humility and lack of pride clearly show that he lives according to the example of Jesus.

7. **He knows that it is more blessed to give than to receive (Acts 20:35).** The servant of the Lord finds happiness in giving to others and putting their needs before his own. He is generous, selfless, and concerned about the welfare of others.

8. **He is _____ when entrusted with something (1 Cor. 4:2).** To the servant of the Lord, there is no such thing as a "too small" task. He delights in serving and proves his faithfulness in the little things that others don't want to do.

9. **He carries the burdens of others (Gal. 6:2).** He has compassion for the needs of others and puts his compassion to work in practical acts of service.

10. **He is _____, gentle, and patient, and he bears with others in love (Eph. 4:2).** He is not easily angered and does not take offense quickly. His life emulates the life of Jesus.

11. **He looks to the interest of others and not just to his own interests (Phil. 2:4).** He is genuinely concerned about others and is not self-absorbed.

12. **He wants to please the Lord in all he does (2 Tim. 2:4).** Like a soldier in an army, he is single-minded. His one focus is to serve his Master and please Him. This is the interior motivation that prompts him to a life of service to others.

Summary: To be great in the kingdom of God is to become a servant. That's the example Jesus gave us, and that is our goal, too. When we allow the Lord to work character, perseverance, and maturity in us through the trials of life, we grow in Christlikeness. As we experience this breaking of self-will, we become less and less preoccupied with ourselves and more and more centered on the needs of others. We look to serve rather than be served, to love rather than be loved, and to give rather than to receive. These are the marks of the Christian who has been broken before God.

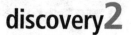

Questions and Discussion Points

1.   Does the way you live reflect your trust in God, or do you act like you need to give Him a hand in running your life?

2.   If you single-mindedly follow God, does that make you narrow-minded? Explain.

3.   If you die to self and live for God, how will that change your life on a daily basis? Why do some people have the mistaken idea that a life lived for God will be difficult, boring, and unfulfilled?

4.   What in your life hinders God from filling you with the Holy Spirit to the measure He desires?

5.   Examine your life. Do you put Jesus first in everything? Can you truly say that you have been crucified with Christ and that you no longer live, but rather Christ lives in you?

6.   Read Joshua 24:14–15. Whom will *you* serve this day?

The Law of Brokenness and Service

Scripture Memory for Discovery 2, Week 10

"The Lord is near to those who have a broken heart, and saves such as have a contrite spirit" (Ps. 34:18 NKJV).

Monday: John 11:17–12:11 _____

_____

_____

Tuesday: John 12:12–13:17 _____

_____

_____

Wednesday: John 13:18–14:31 _____

_____

_____

Thursday: John 15:1–16:33 _____

_____

_____

Friday: John 17:1–18:27 _____

_____

_____

Saturday: John 18:27–19:42 _____

_____

_____

Sunday: John 20:1–21:25 _____

_____

_____

Special Prayer Requests _____

_____

_____

_____

_____

discovery

Conquering Your Land

STAYING *the* COURSE

2

God's Vision for Your Ministry

You cannot conquer your spiritual land unless you are a doer of the Word. Joshua could never have gone in and taken the Promised Land if he had been afraid of doing what God instructed Him to do. But because He obeyed and did the will of the Lord, the land was conquered, just like God had promised him.

Acts 1:1 NASB states, "The first account I composed, Theophilus, about all that Jesus began to *do and teach*" (italics added). Something very significant is mentioned in this passage: Doing and teaching go together! In Luke 24:19 NASB, the Word of God says, "And He said to them, 'What things?' And they said to Him, 'The things about Jesus the Nazarene, who was a prophet *mighty in deed and word* in the sight of God and all the people'" (emphasis added). In both passages, Luke makes it clear that Jesus both *did* and *taught* the ministry. In other words, doing and teaching are the methods that Jesus used to prepare His disciples for a lifetime of fruitful ministry.

In this series of teachings, we will not only teach you in the classroom setting, but more importantly, we'll give you the actual opportunity to put into practice what you are learning. You'll hear about prayer and intercession in the classroom, but more importantly, you'll actually start praying and interceding. You'll also learn about evangelism, but just like with prayer, we'll give you the opportunity to actually do it. It will be the same with serving and all the other ministry aspects that we'll be teaching. You'll learn, and then you'll do.

Jesus' focus was to do the will of the Father. Jesus trained men to do, not just to know. In order for you and me to be successful in ministry, we have to actually do the ministry. After you complete these next ten

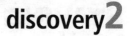

weeks, you will find yourself doing the ministry of Christ: winning souls and making disciples. Like Joshua, you'll walk into your Promised Land and conquer the souls God has waiting for you!

Lesson 1
Praise and Worship

Key Verse: *"But an hour is coming, and now is, when the true worshipers will worship the Father in spirit and truth; for such people the Father seeks to be His worshipers. God is spirit, and those who worship Him must worship in spirit and truth"* (John 4:22–23 NASB).

Key Scriptures:
Hebrews 13:15
Psalm 100:4
Ephesians 5:19–20
Romans 12:1
Colossians 3:16–17
1 Peter 2:9

Objective: The purpose of this lesson is to give the student a clear, biblical understanding of the role of praise and worship in his life.

Introduction: The words *praise and worship* cover the whole of our response of love and appreciation to the Lord. It sums up our entire reason for living (Isa. 43:21; Eph. 1:6, 12, 14). Praise and worship flow naturally from a heart that has been touched by God's love. We thank Him for what He has given us, we praise Him for what He has done for us, and we worship Him for who He is to us.

Psalm 100:4 NIV says, "Enter his gates with thanksgiving and his courts with praise; give thanks to him and praise his name." Paul takes the thought a little further and exhorts us to rejoice in the Lord *always* (Phil. 4:4)!

God loves and cares for us, and He wants us to know this. From grateful hearts, we can give thanks to Him and worship Him in spirit and in truth.

I. _____ in an important aspect of your relationship with God.

A. What is praise?

1. Praise is recognizing who God is (Ps. 104; 1 Chron. 29:10–13).

2. Praise is acknowledging God for all He has done (Ps. 25:8–10; Isa. 25:1).

3. Praise is exalting God (Ps. 34:3; 99:5).

4. Praise is _____ God (Dan. 4:34–37).

5. Praise is magnifying God (Luke 1:46; Acts 10:46).

6. Praise is marveling at God (2 Thess. 1:10).

7. Praise is glorifying God (Rev. 15:4; Ps. 29:1).

B. Why should you praise God?

1. God is enthroned on the praises of His people (Ps. 22:3).

2. Nothing else can praise God quite like man (Ps. 30:9; 115:17–18).

3. Praise lifts up and rejoices in God's great deeds, both now and in the past (Ps. 40:5; 98:1; Ex. 15:6).

4. Praise proclaims God's greatness and majesty to the world (Ps. 66:5–8).

5. Praise releases God's _____ (Ps. 67:5–7).

6. Praise releases God's power (Ps. 149:6–9; 2 Chron. 20:12, 22).

7. God created man (and that means you!) to praise Him (Isa. 43:21; Eph. 1:3–14).

8. You have been instructed to praise God (Eph. 5:18–20; Ps. 100:4; 146:1).

9. Praise is a _____ that pleases God (Heb. 13:15–16; Ps. 107:21–22; 2 Sam. 24:24); it comes from a person's whole being, not just from the lips (Rom. 12:1).

10. God is worthy to receive all praise (Rev. 5:9–14).

C. Praise is a _____.

1. Praise can be a weapon against Satan, your enemy, because he is "allergic" to praise!

2.   In spiritual warfare, you do not keep on praising and singing just for the fun of it. You continue in praise, extolling the Word of God until you sense the anointing of the Holy Spirit (Ps. 56:4, 10–11; 2 Chron. 20:21–22).

3.   Then you persevere until the power of God breaks through (Acts 16:25–26). This kind of praise is not just spoken quietly in your heart, but rather, it is vocal, forceful, and powerful.

II.   _____ is another important aspect of your relationship with God.

A.   What is worship?

1.   Worship = worth + ship, which means appreciating God because He is worthy (Rev. 4:11; 5:12).

    a.   The Hebrew words for "worship" are *segad* and *shachah,* and these mean "to bow down." They also imply the thought of a relationship between a dog and its master, a relationship characterized by adoring love.

    b.   The main Greek word translated as "worship" is *proskuneo,* which means "to kiss the hand" or "to offer homage or reverence."

    c.   Biblical worship, then, has the implied meaning of selfless adoration of a greater being.

2. Jesus shed His blood to give all believers the privilege of worshiping the Father (Heb. 10:19–22).

    a. Through Jesus, you become a priest of God, capable of presenting others to God and God to others (Rev. 1:6; 1 Pet. 2:9).

    b. Worship is an expression of putting God first in your life. When you give to God in this way, He draws you to Himself and gives back to you.

3. Worshiping God is not just singing songs.

    a. Because you are a disciple of Jesus, everything you do (work, pleasure activities, study, family life, and so forth) should be an act of worship to God.

    b. True worship of God involves giving 100 percent of your life to Him, being totally available and totally obedient to Him.

    c. Your worship of God is based on a lifestyle of bringing glory to God.

B. **The Father seeks true worship.**

1. Jesus said, "Yet a time is coming and has now come when the true worshipers will worship the Father in spirit and truth, for they are the kind of worshipers the Father seeks. God is spirit, and his worshipers must worship in spirit and in truth" (John 4:23–24 NIV). This passage teaches five main thoughts:

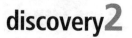
a. **You are expected to worship the Father**—As His redeemed son or daughter, you love Him because He first loved you (1 John 4:19). This should prompt worship to flow from your heart.

b. **You worship from your** _____—This means that you must first be born again of the Holy Spirit if you are to worship God acceptably. Secondly, your worship of God should be led and inspired by the Holy Spirit. Only He knows how to worship God in a way that is pleasing to the Father (1 Cor. 2:10–16; John 16:13–15).

c. **You also worship from your** _____—You worship in truth, out of the reality of a life lived in fellowship with God the Father through Jesus His Son. In fact, the Greek word translated as "truth" is *aletheia,* which also means "reality." Thus true worship is heartfelt; spoken words are useless unless they come from the heart (Matt. 15:8–9). The melody of true praise issues forth from the heart (Eph. 5:19) and brings a joy that only Jesus gives.

d. **You worship with your understanding**—You worship a God that you have come to know personally (John 4:22; Acts 17:22–23; 1 Cor. 14:15).

e. **You worship from the** _____—You do not praise God or worship Him because you feel like it, but because He desires it.

2. Worship is a priority in heaven. Whenever there is a description of God in the Bible, worship is present (Isa. 6:1–5; Rev. 4:6–11; Ezek. 47:1–12).

3. Worship gives place for the rule of God, but the particular form of worship or liturgy (what you do) is not the issue. The issue is whether the life of God is present in your worship.

III. In what ways can you offer praise and worship to God?

A.   You can praise with _____ (Ps. 9:1).

B.   You can shout (Ps. 95:1).

C.   You can bow down (Ps. 95:6).

D.   You can _____ (Ps. 33:1; 104:33).

E.   You can dance before Him (Ps. 149:3; 150:4).

        1.   This is a symbol of the larger truth that your whole life—body, soul, and spirit—is surrendered to the Lord in response to His love.

        2.   Spiritual dance indicates surrender, humility, and abandon to God. It seeks to worship God unabashedly, not deterred by the opinions of others.

F.   You can raise your hands to Him (Ps. 134:2).

        1.   When you raise your hands to your heavenly Father, you are expressing love and dependence, much like a baby does when it raises its hands to its natural father or mother.

        2.   The raising of the hands can also be a victory proclamation in the Lord.

G. You can praise with instruments, with or without singing (Ps. 98:4–6; 150: 3–5).

H. Your _____ _____ can be an act of praise (Rom. 12:1; Phil. 1:20; 1 Cor. 6:20; Eph. 5:20; 1 Thess. 5:16–18).

I. You can sing with the Spirit in a God-given language (1 Cor. 14:15).

J. You can praise with psalms, hymns, or spiritual songs (Eph. 5:19–20).

   1. Singing with psalms means singing the Word of God, especially the psalms.

   2. Hymns are special compositions written to exalt Jesus as Lord and God in His greatness.

   3. Spiritual songs are original songs prepared in advance or spontaneously inspired by the Holy Spirit. They express your experience of the Lord.

Summary: Christians have the awesome privilege of praising and worshiping the God of the universe. In fact, that is the central thrust of our lives. Praise and worship are so essential because they are a reflection of what is in our hearts. If we are filled with love, appreciation, and gratitude, our words will reveal that. We can't help but overflow with thanksgiving and praise to the Father.

If our worship of God stems from duty, rote, and meaningless tradition, then it will be weak and ineffective. God is looking for those who will worship Him in spirit and in truth. To those, He will reveal Himself.

Questions and Discussion Points

1. Should you thank God for all He does for you? Do you actually do so?

2. Why should you live a lifestyle where praise and worship are central?

3. Did you know that God sings? Read Zephaniah 3:17 and discuss what it means.

4. In what ways do you praise and worship the Lord? Are there ways of worship that you have held back from? What is keeping you from praising Him with all your mind, body, and spirit?

5. When you worship God, do you simply sing songs, or do you worship Him in spirit and in truth? How can you tell the difference?

6. How far have you gone with the Lord in your praise and worship? Examine your heart, and purpose to worship with all your being.

Lesson 2
Spiritual Warfare

Key Verse: *"Be of sober spirit, be on the alert. Your adversary, the devil, prowls around like a roaring lion, seeking someone to devour. But resist him, firm in your faith, knowing that the same experiences of suffering are being accomplished by your brethren who are in the world"* (1 Peter 5:8–9 NASB).

Key Scriptures:
Ephesians 1:17–23; 6:10–18
Revelation 12:10–11
2 Corinthians 4:4
Luke 11:14–26
James 4:7
Colossians 2:15

Objective: The goal of this lesson is to teach the student how to fight and win against Satan.

Introduction: When we are born again, we cross over from the kingdom of darkness into the kingdom of God (or the kingdom of light). Once we served Satan (John 8:42–47), but now we serve God because He rescued us from the dominion of Satan (Col. 1:12–14). Satan is not pleased that we no longer serve him. In fact, he will try to do everything possible to get us to fall and come under his dominion again. For this reason, we must learn how to resist Satan's advances and stand in the victory that Jesus won over Satan and his demonic forces.

We must also learn spiritual warfare in order to fulfill our commission to make disciples of all nations. The people in the world are under the power of Satan (2 Cor. 4:4) and cannot see the truth. Before they can come to Christ, we need to release the power of God for salvation to deliver them from the kingdom of darkness and bring them into the kingdom of God.

We do not have to defeat Satan again. Jesus has already won a total victory (Col. 2:15); we just need to enforce that victory. As we engage in spiritual warfare, we enable God to use us to bring others into the light of God's kingdom.

I.   There is a spiritual battleground with two opposing sides.

A.   One side is the kingdom of _____.

1.   The kingdom of God is the powerful rule and reign of God over all of life. It is sometimes referred to as the kingdom of heaven or the kingdom of light.

2.   Jesus preached the kingdom of God as the Good News of His message (Mark 1:15; Matt. 4:23), and the apostles followed suit (Acts 8:12).

3.   God's kingdom comes with power to save, change, heal, and deliver from demons (Matt. 4:23; 9:35; 12:28; Mark 16:15–18).

4.   This power comes from the Holy Spirit, who imparts the righteousness, peace, and joy of God (Rom. 14:17; 1 Cor. 4:20).

B.   The opposing side is the kingdom of _____.

1. Satan and his angels' rebellion produced a kingdom set up in opposition to God.

2. Through Satan's enticing of Adam and Eve, sin entered the world. The devil continues to draw all human beings into sin and his kingdom of darkness.

3. As a Christian, your fight is against the evil forces of darkness (Eph. 6:12), and your main adversary is Satan.

C.   Who is Satan?

1. Satan is a real being (Luke 4:1–13), not just a figment of the imagination. Originally, he was a beautiful angel called Lucifer, but he was cast out of heaven because of his pride (Isa. 14:11–15; Ezek. 28:12–17).

2. The Bible uses many different terms to describe Satan. Some of these terms are listed below:

   a. He is called "your enemy, the devil" (1 Pet. 5:8 NIV).

   b. He is "the tempter" (1 Thess. 3:5 NKJV).

   c. He is "the father of _____" (John 8:44 NIV).

   d. He is called "the ruler of the kingdom of the air" (Eph. 2:2 NIV).

   e. He is also referred to as "the evil one" (1 John 2:14 NIV).

   f. He is "the _____ of our brethren" (Rev. 12:10 NKJV).

g.   He is "a murderer" (John 8:44).

h.   He was first referred to as "the serpent" (Gen. 3:1).

i.   He is also called "an angel of light" (2 Cor. 11:14).

3.   At the present time, the entire world system is in Satan's grip (1 John 5:19). He is the ultimate source of sin, sickness, and death.

4.   He has a kingdom of demons (Matt. 12:24–28) composed of evil spirits (Luke 11:24–26), or fallen angels (Matt. 25:41). These are intelligent, active beings that dwell on earth and in supernatural realms (Eph. 6:11–12).

5.   Remember: The devil, or Satan, is not equal with God or even effective against God. He is not all-knowing or all-powerful.

D.   How does the enemy attack?

1.   You cannot afford to be ignorant of Satan's evil schemes (2 Cor. 2:11). You must be aware that the devil is constantly out to destroy you (1 Pet. 5:8). He is clever and cunning in his tactics (Eph. 6:11; Gen. 3:1–6), and he will try anything at any time to pull you down.

2.   The main battlefield is in your _____. Satan accuses (Zech. 3:1), deceives (2 Cor. 11:14), tempts (1 Thess. 3:5), and lies (John 8:44). He inspires evil thoughts, confusion, complacency, laziness, doubt, fear, despair, unbelief, and discouragement. He appeals to your fleshly desires and will try to entice you through idolatry, witchcraft, or other occult practices.

3. Satan also uses his fallen angels, called demons, to trouble and torment people (Luke 13:10–16).

II. You can be victorious over Satan.

A. Jesus overcame Satan.

1. He deterred him with the _____ _____ _____ (Matt. 4:4).

2. He delivered those Satan had oppressed with sickness (Acts 10:38).

3. He demonstrated the superior power of the Holy Spirit and the kingdom of God (Matt. 12:28).

4. He totally defeated Satan and all his hosts through His death on the cross (Col. 2:15; Heb. 2:14).

5. He sealed Satan's destiny, once and for all (Matt. 25: 41).

6. Jesus shares His victory with His people, giving them the authority to defeat Satan in their own lives. The reason the Son of God appeared was to destroy the works of the devil (1 John 3:8).

B. You can overcome Satan.

1. Jesus said that in His name, His disciples would drive out demons as part of their work for Him (Mark 16:16–17). Your strategy for warfare, whether for yourself or for others, consists of several steps.

   a. First, you must _____ Satan's activities (2 Cor. 2:11).

   b. Then, you _____ his advances (Eph. 4:27).

   c. Next, you _____ his attacks (James 4:7; 1 Pet. 5:8–9).

   d. Finally, you must recognize where God is at work and do as God directs you to do in the situation.

2. You can use your spiritual armor to defend yourself against the enemy.

   a. The blood of Jesus cleanses you from all sin when you confess your sin to God and receive His forgiveness (1 John 1:7–9). The blood of Jesus also enables you to live in victory over Satan (Rev. 12:11; Col. 2:15). If you live in the blessing of this provision of God, Satan will not be able to gain a foothold in your life.

   b. You must put on the full armor of God in order to stand your ground regardless of what the enemy throws at you. Putting on this armor is like putting on the Lord Jesus (Rom. 13:14). The armor of God is divided into a number of items (Eph. 6:10–18). Check to see if you are wearing your spiritual armor.

      (1) **Are you wearing the belt of _____?**—Do you live in the truth and in God's reality? Jesus is the truth, dwelling in you and inspiring you to live a truthful life (John 14:6).

(2) **Have you put on the breastplate of righteousness?**—Are you living righteously before God? Jesus is your righteousness, inspiring you to righteous living (2 Cor. 5:21).

(3) **Are your feet fitted with the readiness that comes from the Gospel of peace?**—Are you fulfilling the Great Commission to go and make disciples of all nations? Jesus is the Prince of Peace (Isa. 9:6), and you carry His Gospel.

(4) **Have you taken up the shield of _____?**—Are you living a life of faith, trusting in God and knowing your victory over the enemy and your flesh? Jesus is the author and finisher of your faith (Heb. 12:2).

(5) **Have you put on the helmet of salvation?**—Do you know that you are born again and are a child of God? Jesus is the captain and author of your salvation (Heb. 2:10).

(6) **Have you taken up the sword of the Spirit?**—Do you know the Word of God and what it says about who you are in Christ? Jesus is the living Word, and He has given you His Word as an active weapon in your mouth (Heb. 4:12; John 1:14).

(7) **Do you pray in the Spirit on all occasions?**—Are you open to the Holy Spirit's leading and prompting, and do you know how to pray effectively? Jesus gives you access to the Father, and you can therefore present things to Him in Jesus' name (Heb. 4:16; John 14:13).

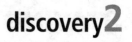

3.	When Satan has someone in his grip or when he comes against you personally, you have the authority to not only defend yourself, but also to go on the offensive. Some of the offensive weapons you can use are listed below:

　　a.	The _____ _____ _____ has power over everything in heaven and earth. Demons are subject to it and cannot resist it (Acts 16:18; Phil. 2:9–10).

　　b.	The Word of God within you gives you strength to overcome the devil. It is a spiritual weapon, full of divine power (1 John 2:14; Eph. 6:17).

　　c.	The power of the Spirit gives you victory over demonic attack (Acts 10:38). Without the presence of the Spirit, you will be weak and ineffective against the devil's attacks.

4.	The victory is assured: "Thanks be to God! He gives us the victory through our Lord Jesus Christ" (1 Cor. 15:57 NIV).

　　a.	Everything is placed under the feet of Jesus Christ because He rules over all (Eph. 1:21–23), and furthermore, He gives His authority to all believers (Matt. 10:1; 28:18–20; Rom. 16:20).

　　b.	Because you are born of God, you are kept safe (Rom. 8:37–39).

　　c.	He who is in you, Christ Jesus, is greater than he who is in the world, Satan (1 John 4:4).

　　d.	There is overcoming power in the blood of Jesus and in your _____ of Him (Rev. 12:11).

e.   When you resist the devil and are submitted to God, the devil will flee (James 4:7).

f.   Jesus declared, "I tell you the truth, anyone who has faith in me will do what I have been doing. He will do even greater things than these, because I am going to the Father" (John 14:12 NIV).

Summary: During our earthly journey, we have a very real enemy. Satan, the enemy of our souls, will stop at nothing to keep us from turning to Christ. He knows that he is a defeated foe to those who surrender their hearts and lives to Jesus.

When Jesus died on the cross and rose again from the dead, Satan's defeat was final and complete. Because of Jesus' victory, Christians share in this triumph over the devil and the kingdom of darkness. Once we understand that and begin walking in it, we will discover the secret of living victoriously in Christ.

Questions and Discussion Points

1.   Why don't people in the world understand the truth of the Gospel? (See 2 Corinthians 4:4.)

2.   If Christ Jesus won such a complete victory for us, why do so many Christians seem to be living in defeat?

3.   Why do you think Satan attacks people? If you are doing nothing for God, do you think Satan will still attack? Discuss.

4.   Is there any area of your life in which you are allowing Satan a foothold?

5.   Have you checked to make sure you are wearing all your spiritual armor? Put it on, and then stand and face Satan boldly. Don't ever run from him, remembering that the armor Paul wrote about had no protection for the back!

6.   Do you live as a victorious child of God, overcoming Satan and all his wicked schemes? If not, why not? What could you do to more effectively walk in the victory that is yours through Christ?

Lesson 3
The Power of Intercession

Key Verse: *"And He saw that there was no man, and was astonished that there was no one to intercede; then His own arm brought salvation to Him, and His righteousness upheld Him"* (Isa. 59:16 NASB).

Key Scriptures:
Ezekiel 22:30
Job 9:32–33
Hebrews 4:16; 7:25
1 Timothy 2:1–6
2 Chronicles 7:14
Romans 8:26–27
Genesis 18:16–33
1 John 5:14–15

Objective: Through this lesson, the student will learn much about intercession: (1) the definition of intercession, (2) the biblical basis of intercession, (3) Jesus Christ as the model for intercession, (4) how to do intercession, and (5) the importance of intercession.

Introduction: *Merriam Webster's Collegiate Dictionary, Eleventh Edition* defines the word *intercession* as "the act of interceding," and "prayer, petition, or entreaty in favor of another." The *Full Life Bible* defines it as "holy, believing, persevering prayer whereby someone pleads with God on behalf of another or others who desperately need God's intervention."

God is searching for those who will be intercessors, those who can actually change life situations and people through their fervent, upright prayers. He has chosen us to be colaborers with Him, giving us the tremendous privilege of reconciling men, women, and children to the Father.

I.   Scripture provides many examples of intercessors.

A.   _____ was an intercessor (Gen. 18:16–33).

1.   Abraham made time for the Lord to speak to him (Gen. 18:1–3). By opening the door to the Lord and sitting down with Him, Abraham had the chance to hear the heart of God.

2.   Abraham felt the horror of what was about to happen to Sodom and Gomorrah, and it motivated him to intercede. Abraham asked God specifically for souls. His prayer was effective, and consequently, Lot and his daughters were spared.

2.   If you are wrapped up only in yourself, you will never be a great intercessor. Every lost person faces an eternity in hell. Every sinner is in the same state you were in before you found grace. Every hurting person is somebody's family member or somebody's friend. You must start seeing beyond yourself and concern yourself with others.

B.   Esther was another intercessor (Esther 4:10–16).

1.   Esther assumed a dangerous position when she stood in the gap for her own people. She identified with them in their plight. She experienced the agony of that identification:

"My maids and I will fast likewise. And so I will go to the king, which is against the law; and if I perish, I perish!" (Esther 4:16 NKJV).

2. Because of her courageous decision, she gained a place of authority before the king: "What is your petition, Queen Esther? It shall be granted you. And what is your request, up to half the kingdom? It shall be done!" (Esther 7:2 NKJV).

C. Daniel was an intercessor (Dan. 9:1–27; 10:2–3).

1. Daniel fasted and sought God in deep intercession for twenty-one days because of Israel's enslavement and captivity in Babylon following the destruction of Jerusalem and the temple.

2. Daniel expected and anticipated an answer from the Lord regarding his prayers.

D. _____, too, was an intercessor (Ex. 8:8–12).

1. In the Bible, the first mention of intercession occurs when Pharaoh asks Moses to entreat God to stop the plague of frogs. Moses replies, "Accept the honor of saying when I shall intercede for you, for your servants, and for your people, to destroy the frogs from you and your houses, that they may remain in the river only" (v. 9 NKJV).

2. Verses 12 and 13 say, "And Moses cried out to the Lord concerning the frogs which he had brought against Pharaoh. So the Lord did according to the word of Moses. And the frogs died out of the houses, out of the courtyards, and out of the fields."

3. From this account in Exodus 8, we can see certain key principles regarding intercession.

a.   There is a gap between the subject and God.

b.   The intercessor identifies with the subject.

c.   The intercessor identifies with God.

d.   The intercessor cries out to the Lord, entreating Him on behalf of the subject.

e.   The intercessor attains a place of authority in the situation.

E.   Jesus Christ is the greatest _____ of all (1 Tim. 2:5; Heb. 7:25; Rom. 8:34).

1.   Jesus was an intercessor while He was here on earth. He prayed for those who were sick and possessed by demons. He prayed for His disciples. He even prayed for you when He interceded for all those who would believe in Him (John 17:20).

2.   Jesus continued His ministry of intercession after His death and resurrection and ascension into heaven. He now serves as your great intercessor in heaven.

3.   Your prayers can move the hand of God and release the reconciling work of the Holy Spirit. God has designed it to be so, perhaps for two reasons: that you might learn how very dependent you are upon Him, and that He might be able to share the burden, grief, and joy of His own heart with you.

II.   There is a strong biblical basis for your intercession.

A. **You are a part of the _____ of believers (1 Pet. 2:9).**

1. The biblical basis for your ministry of intercessory prayer is your calling as a priest unto God.

2. The Word of God declares that believers are a holy priesthood (1 Pet. 2:5), a royal priesthood (1 Pet. 2:9), and a kingdom of priests (Rev. 1:5). As part of the body of Christ, that is your calling, too.

B. **You are called to offer spiritual sacrifices to God (1 Pet. 2:5).**

1. The background for understanding your calling to priestly intercession is found in the Old Testament example of the Levitical priesthood.

2. The priest's responsibility was to stand *before* and *between*. He stood *before* God to minister to Him with sacrifices and offerings, and he stood *between* a righteous God and sinful man, bringing them together at the place of the blood sacrifice.

C. **You are a _____ for the intercessory prayer of the Holy Spirit (Rom. 8:26).**

D. **You are called to intercede for your nation (2 Chron. 7:14).**

III. **Here are some principles for effective intercession.**

A. **Offer _____ to God.**

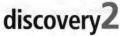
1. Praise God for who He is and for the privilege of engaging in the same wonderful ministry as the Lord Jesus (Heb. 7:25).

2. Praise God for the privilege of cooperating with Him in the affairs of men through prayer.

B.   Make sure your heart is clean before God.

1. Give the Holy Spirit opportunity to convict you of any unconfessed sin (Ps. 66:18; 139:23–24).

2. Confess and repent of anything He brings to mind.

C.   Deal aggressively with the enemy.

1. Come against him in the all-powerful name of the Lord Jesus Christ (Mark 16:17). Actively resist him (James 4:7).

2. Use the sword of the Spirit, the Word of God, as a weapon (Eph. 6:17; Heb. 4:12).

D.   Approach God in _____.

1. Praise God in faith for the remarkable prayer time you are about to have.

2. God is a remarkable God and will do something consistent with His character.

E.   _____ before God.

1.   Wait before God in silent expectancy (Ps. 62:5; Mic. 7:7).

2.   Listen for His direction (Ps. 81:13–14).

F.   In obedience and faith, continue asking God for direction.

1.   As one of God's flock, you belong to Him. You will hear His voice as you seek Him (John 10:27).

2.   Expect God to give you direction. He will (Ps. 32:8).

3.   Be encouraged by the lives of Moses, Daniel, Paul, and Anna, knowing that God gives revelation to those who make intercession a way of life.

G.   Keep your Bible near.

1.   If possible, have your Bible with you in case God wants to give you direction or confirmation from His Word (Ps. 119:105).

2.   Be quick to obey the Word of the Lord.

H.   Intercede, using the promises of God (1 John 5:14–15).

I.   If possible, intercede with a partner (Matt. 18:19).

Summary: Intercessors participate with God in the affairs of men and nations. Through their prayers, the lost come to Christ, the sick are healed, and the oppressed are set free. Intercession is powerful, mighty, and effective to the pulling down of strongholds.

All Christians are priests before the Lord, and as priests, they have the right and responsibility to stand before God on behalf of others. Their intercession can change the course of individual lives as well as the course of nations. For reasons we may not fully understand, God has designed it to be so.

Intercessors are people of prayer and power. They are worshipers who seek God's face. Because of their intimate relationship with Him, He reveals His heart and sometimes His secrets to them. The call to intercession is for everyone who wants to discover the joy of laboring with God on behalf of others. The call to intercession is for *you!*

Questions and Discussion Points

1. What does it mean to intercede in prayer?

2. Summarize some of the principles of effective intercession that you learned in this lesson.

3. Explain how you can use the promises of God to intercede in prayer.

4. Why are intercessors often worshipers? Discuss the relationship between intercession and worship.

5. Have you ever interceded for someone or a particular situation and seen God move? Share what happened.

Lesson 4
Prayer and Cells

Key Verse: *"Therefore, confess your sins to one another, and pray for one another so that you may be healed. The effective prayer of a righteous man can accomplish much. Elijah was a man with a nature like ours, and he prayed earnestly that it would not rain, and it did not rain on the earth for three years and six months. Then he prayed again, and the sky poured rain and the earth produced its fruit"* (James 5:16–18 NASB).

Key Scriptures:
Luke 18:1–8
2 Corinthians 4:4
1 Timothy 2:4
2 Timothy 2:25

Objective: The goal of this lesson is to teach the student how to develop a prayer life focused on seeing others come to know Jesus Christ.

Introduction: The power of prayer is unquestionable. Lost souls come to Christ, sick bodies are made whole, broken marriages are restored, and financial lack becomes provision when fervent prayer is released in the heavenlies.

There are different types of prayer, each with a specific function. You are probably already familiar with fellowship prayer, where you spend intimate time alone in God's presence, enjoying His company and drawing near to Him. This lesson will concentrate on another type of prayer: task prayer. In particular, we'll examine how we can use this type of prayer to bring souls into the kingdom of God.

I. Task prayer is prayer for a specific goal, in particular, a goal that requires divine intervention (James 5:16–18).

A. Task prayer is different from fellowship prayer.

1. Elijah prayed both effectually and fervently. He bowed seven times toward the Mediterranean Sea and did not stop until he saw a cloud rising from the waters (1 Kings 18:41–46). This is an example of task prayer.

2. Dr. Paul Yongii Cho teaches the difference between task prayer and fellowship prayer. He prays through the "tabernacle prayer" each day in his private prayer time, using the various parts and articles of the tabernacle as reference points for prayer. When he reaches the Holy of Holies, however, he prays task prayer over areas in which he needs miraculous intervention.

B. The prayer of the persistent widow illustrates task prayer (Luke 18:1–8).

1. Christ taught us to pray and not give up. The story of the widow in Luke 18 illustrates the tenacious spirit necessary to pray a miracle into existence.

2. The widow's words were strong and persistent. She said, "Avenge me of mine adversary" (v. 3 KJV). The key to her success was in her continual coming to the judge with her

petition. Like a hammer hitting a nail, she drove her point home until the unjust judge was finally willing to grant the petition, simply for the sake of gaining relief.

3. If this unjust judge finally conceded to the widow's request, how much more will our just and good God grant us our requests when we pray unceasingly and fervently!

C.   Prayer for _____ is task prayer.

1. As a believer, you must begin to cry out to God for those who are lost, sick, and bound.

2. Effectual, fervent prayer will open the heavens and set them free.

II.   You can use the "_____ _____ _____" to pray in the harvest (James 5:19–20).

A.   Select the names of three unsaved people.

1. All evangelism should first begin with specific, targeted prayer. The prayer of three is a technique that zeros in on prayer for three particular people to be saved.

2. As your cell follows through with the prayer of three, you will see amazing results in the number of souls being saved.

3. In using the prayer of three, each cell member first writes down the names of three people who need Christ: family, coworkers, or other contacts.

B.   **First step: _____ one day a week for those three people.**

    1.   Each cell member should fast one day a week for a month for the salvation of those three people. Fasting may be done all day until the evening meal, if desired.

    2.   This will break down the hold of the powers of darkness and will allow the Gospel to penetrate.

C.   **Second step: Quote _____ daily over the three.**

    1.   Example: 2 Corinthians 4:4—"Lord, I command the blinding spirits over (insert name of one of your three) to release his/her mind and that the light of the Gospel of Christ would shine unto him/her."

    2.   Example: 1 Timothy 2:4—"Lord, You desire all men to be saved and to come unto the knowledge of the truth. Let Your will be done in (insert name of one of your three), and give him/her repentance."

    3.   Example: 2 Timothy 2:25—"Lord, give (insert name of one of your three) repentance to the acknowledging of the truth that he/she would come to his/her senses and escape the trap of the devil."

D.   **Third step: Discern their spiritual _____.**

    1.   Satan has certain strongholds in lost people. The Holy Spirit wants to reveal their true needs and the arguments and logic that keep them from salvation.

2. You must be able to discern for your three whether intellectualism, disappointment, confusion, addiction, or some other area is keeping them from receiving the Gospel. Then you can pray more effectively for them.

E.   Fourth step: Invite them to a private time.

1. After praying the Word, fasting, and discerning their needs for twenty-one days, call them and talk to them. Invite them to spend some private time with you at a meal, over coffee, or in any type of informal setting.

2. Don't mention anything about wanting to witness to them. Simply concentrate on building relationships with them. If, however, they bring up the subject of the Lord, you may go ahead and minister the Gospel to them.

F.   Fifth step: Invite them to a second meeting the next week.

1. At this second meeting, tell them you have been praying for them. Now ask them if there is anything specific for which they would like prayer. Hopefully, they are now ready to receive the Lord and to be plugged into your cell group.

2. Prayer will literally fill any cell in this way!

G.   Last step: Bring them to church.

1. This is the vision: souls and cells. Unless cells are winning souls, the vision will die.

2.   Every cell should be committed to winning souls. As people get saved in the cells, new converts should be brought to the altar in a service for a public confession of faith. They should be encouraged to get water baptized and to attend an Encounter. The goal is to effectively connect them to the church.

Summary: Prayer is the key to seeing the lost come to Christ. When we use the prayer of three to target the lost, we are concentrating all our efforts into task prayer that brings salvation. Any cell will grow when the prayer of three is used as a compassionate tool of ministry. It provides a spiritual focus and an easy-to-follow plan of reaching out to the lost. Don't neglect this dynamic tool of ministry!

Questions and Discussion Points

1.   What is the difference between task prayer and tabernacle prayer?

2.   How did the widow gain justice from the unjust judge? What does this teach us about prayer?

3.   Who are the three people that you are believing God to save? Have you begun the prayer of three concerning them?

4.   Share with your cell what you learned from this lesson, and ask the cell to begin the prayer of three for new souls to be added.

Lesson 5
The Value of a Soul

Key Verse: *"For what will it profit a man if he gains the whole world, and loses his own soul?"* (Mark 8:36 NKJV).

Key Scriptures:

Genesis 2:7
Ezekiel 18:4
Ecclesiastes 12:7
Galatians 4:4–5
1 Peter 2:25; 5:8
John 3:16
1 John 4:9
Matthew 26:37–39; 27:26–31
Isaiah 53:3–7
Job 1:8–11
2 Corinthians 4:3–4

Objective: This lesson will explain the value of a soul in the eyes of God.

Introduction: Throughout world history, kings, dictators, and other rulers have possessed untold riches, fame, and power. They have been acclaimed and even idolized, as though they were somehow different from

everyone else. But upon their deaths, none of that mattered. Like everyone else, they departed this earthly life and faced an eternal destination of either heaven or hell.

Worldly life and its pleasures are fleeting; only the soul (spirit) lasts forever. It follows, therefore, that only the soul has eternal value, and it should be our focus and emphasis while we are upon the earth.

I. God holds the human soul in high esteem.

A. Every soul has its origin in God.

1. God recognizes the soul from the time of its conception (Ps. 139:14–16).

2. We are made in the image of God, our lives initiated by His breath (Gen. 2:7). God seeks to reconcile humanity to Himself.

3. The Bible says that every soul belongs to God. Therefore, God has the right to judge and to forgive (Ezek. 18:4).

4. Our souls will one day return to God (Eccles. 12:7).

B. The _____ of a soul proves its worth.

1. Sin separates the soul from God (Isa. 59:2). God, however, provided a way to bridge the gap that exists between Him and sinful humanity.

2. What is it that made it possible for man's soul to be rescued from the dominion of sin? Romans 5:6–8 NKJV provides the answer: "For when we were still without strength, in due time Christ died for the ungodly. For scarcely for a righteous man will one die; yet perhaps for a good man someone would even dare to die. But God demonstrates His own love toward us, in that while we were still sinners, Christ died for us."

3. Man was not redeemed by cheap religion. First Peter 1:18–20 NIV says, "For you know that it was not with perishable things such as silver or gold that you were redeemed from the empty way of life handed down to you from your forefathers, but with the precious blood of Christ, a lamb without blemish or defect. He was chosen before the creation of the world, but was revealed in these last times for your sake."

C. God provides a way for lost souls to come back to Him.

1. God devised a plan and sent Jesus to be a ransom for many (Gal. 4:4–5).

2. Jesus is the Shepherd (1 Pet. 2:25) and is willing to leave the ninety-nine to seek out the one lost sheep (Luke 15: 3–7).

3. The angels in heaven rejoice over one soul that repents and comes back to the Father (Luke 15:10).

D. God gave heaven's fairest jewel to rescue lost humanity.

1. God knew that the only way to make a pathway to heaven for us was to give the life of His only begotten Son (John 3:16). There was nothing of more value to Him than His Son; yet He gave Him up for us. This proves our worth.

2.   "This is how God showed his love among us: He sent his one and only Son into the world that we might live through him" (1 John 4:9 NIV).

II.   Satan tries to _____ every soul.

A.   Satan does not like to see people loving and serving God (Job 1:8–11).

1.   Satan can't stand to see someone in right relationship with God. He does not want people to know, love, and serve God. His intention for all humanity is to lead them away from God and thus condemn them to an eternity in hell.

2.   If our souls were not valuable, then Satan would not involve himself in our affairs. The very fact that he comes after us with all he's got shows how valuable we are.

B.   _____ _____ is safe from the devil's attack; he will try to get everyone he can (John 10:10).

1.   Even Peter was a target for the enemy (Luke 22:31–32). Being part of Jesus' select group of disciples did not inoculate him from attack. In fact, it may well have increased it! In the same way, being a Christian certainly does not mean that the devil will not attack you; he will probably attack you all the more.

2.   The enemy is a devourer; he seeks to destroy (1 Pet. 5:8). That is his intent for you: destruction on every level. He wants your health, prosperity, joy, peace, and especially your spiritual destination.

3.   The enemy wants to ensnare you (1 Tim. 3:7). He will use every subtle attack at his disposal to cause you to doubt God and turn away from Him. He will whisper lies to you, bring discouragement, and make you feel rejected. His ways of attack are truly endless.

C.   **Satan wants the lost to remain _____ to the truth (2 Cor. 4:3–4).**

1.   Satan is a great deceiver. He blinds the minds of those who don't know Christ, hoping to keep them from a saving knowledge of the truth.

2.   It is as though there is a veil over their eyes. Until that veil is removed, they cannot see Christ or their need for Him.

III.   Christ knew the value of a soul and willingly became a ransom for us.

A.   **Jesus knew the _____ that had to be paid (Matt. 26:37–39).**

1.   While in the Garden of Gethsemane, Jesus came to terms with the cost of redeeming humanity.

2.   He wrestled with the tremendous cost of obeying the will of God; yet He willingly surrendered and gave 100 percent: His own life.

B.   **He did not suffer and die just to save "junk" (Matt. 27:26–31).**

1.   The name *Barabbas* means "a father's son." Barabbas was a notorious criminal, deserving of death. Had it not been for Jesus, Barabbas would never have been set free.

2. This is a perfect picture of divine grace: the upright as a ransom for the transgressor, the just for the unjust.

3. We are all "Barabbas." We deserve death, but Jesus gave His life that we might go free. This proves the high value He attaches to our souls.

C. He willingly paid the awful price for our souls (Isa. 53:3–7).

1. This descriptive passage from Isaiah records the brutal treatment Jesus suffered for all of us. Words such as *despised, rejected, smitten, afflicted, pierced,* and *crushed* all reveal how much He suffered for us.

2. No one should ever be able to persuade you that you don't matter, that your life has no eternal value. God sent His Son to die a horrible death in your place. The Son willingly surrendered His place in heaven to become the sacrificial Lamb of God. What further proof do you need?

Summary: The only truly valuable possession any of us have is our soul. We take nothing else with us when we depart this life. It is the only thing we have that has eternal value. Both God and Satan know the value of a soul, but we determine its eternal destination.

The soul is so valuable that God gave His only Son, Jesus, to reconcile lost sinners to Himself. That fact alone is enough to stop any argument against the worth of a human being. We are precious, valuable, and cherished, and the God of the universe wants us with Him in heaven for eternity. That's how much we mean to Him!

Questions and Discussion Points

1. What is the most valuable item you possess? To what lengths do you go to protect it? If you lost it, what would you do?

2. How would you feel if one of your children were physically lost? What would you do in order to find your child?

3. God went to great expense to redeem you. What does that tell you about how valuable you are to Him?

4. Now that you realize the battle that is being waged over your soul, what can you do to prevent the enemy from bringing you into any kind of bondage?

D.   He came to save the world (John 3:17).

1.   "For God did not send his Son into the world to condemn the world, but to save the world through him" (NIV).

2.   Jesus offers salvation. That is His entire purpose and desire. He did not come to condemn, but to save the world through His death and resurrection.

III.   Without Christ, the world is lost and hopeless.

A.   All humanity is _____ in trespasses and sins (Eph 2:1).

1.   From the time of the Fall in the Garden of Eden, all humanity has been hopelessly under the curse of sin and death. From Adam and Eve, we have inherited a basic nature of sin that dwells in us from birth.

2.   In this fallen condition, we are "doomed forever," as the NLT says. Within us, we have no power to remedy the situation. Good works, intriguing philosophy, religious ritual, vain traditions—no manmade thing can rescue us from our sins.

B.   Without exception, all have sinned (Rom 3:10, 23).

1.   "As it is written, There is none righteous, no, not one" (v. 10 KJV). That verse makes it clear that no one can justify himself before God. Every man, woman, and child who ever walked the face of this earth is a sinner.

2. "For all have sinned; all fall short of God's glorious standard" (v. 23 NLT). God has a standard of righteousness to which no one can measure up. It doesn't matter how good, loving, and kind a person may seem; in God's eyes, he will always come up short, because he is not perfect. Perfection is not possible for any human being.

C. Unless we have the life of Christ within us, we stand _____ (John 3:18).

1. "Whoever believes in him is not condemned, but whoever does not believe stands condemned already because he has not believed in the name of God's one and only Son" (NIV).

2. Jesus came to save us, not condemn us. However, if we refuse His salvation and lordship, we condemn ourselves.

D. Apart from Christ, we are "harassed and helpless, like sheep without a shepherd" (Matt. 9:36 NIV).

1. Sheep without a shepherd are scattered and fearful. They are left to their own devices and are thus vulnerable to attack.

2. The NLT gives further insight into our condition apart from Christ. That translation says this: "Their problems were so great and they didn't know where to go for help." That's how we are without Christ: totally overwhelmed, with no one to help us and no place to go for help.

E. There are _____ upon _____ of souls who do not know Christ (Matt. 9:37).

    1.   "The harvest truly is plentiful, but the laborers are few" (NKJV). Untold millions do not know Christ. Some have never even heard His name. Unless laborers go into the harvest fields of the world, they will be forever lost to an eternity in hell.

    2.   We who know Christ are the laborers called to work in the harvest. The lost cannot call upon Him unless they have believed; they cannot believe unless they have heard; they cannot hear unless someone preaches to them; and we cannot preach unless we will go to them (Rom. 10:14–15).

F. The harvest is ripe (John 4:35).

    1.   "Lift up your eyes and look at the fields, for they are already white for harvest!" (NIV). Many, many people are ready to receive Christ if given the opportunity. A vast spiritual harvest waits; only the laborers are lacking.

    2.   Eternal souls are the harvest. At times we plant seeds into the lives of others, and at other times, we have the wonderful privilege of reaping from the work that others have done (vv. 36–38). Regardless of the specific role we play, we must be busy in the Father's work of harvest.

G. The workers are few (Matt. 9:37).

    1.   "The harvest is plentiful but the workers are few. Ask the Lord of the harvest, therefore, to send out workers into his harvest field" (vv. 37–38 NIV).

2. Very few workers are available for bringing in the vast harvest. Some people are simply unwilling, while others feel incapable, but the responsibility, nevertheless, rests with us who call ourselves Christians. If we don't do it, it will not get done.

IV. Jesus gave us five specific commands to fulfilling the Great Commission.

A. "Therefore _____ and make disciples of all nations" (Matt. 28:19–20 NIV).

B. "_____ the Gospel to every creature" (Mark 16:15 KJV).

C. "_____ and forgiveness of sins will be preached in his name" (Luke 24:47 NIV).

D. "As the Father has sent Me, I also _____ you" (John 20:21 NKJV).

E. "You shall be _____ to Me" (Acts 1:8 NKJV).

Summary: Since Christ died for all and it is God's will that none should perish, He has commissioned the church to take the Gospel to all creation. This is a standing commandment in effect until Christ returns. No Christian is exempt from the responsibility of taking the Gospel to the lost. Evangelism is not a task relegated solely to the professional clergy or to those who proclaim themselves "evangelists." We will all give an account for what we have done with our earthly lives, including our obedience to Christ's command to preach the Gospel and make disciples.

Questions and Discussion Points

1. What is the proof of God's love for sinners?

2. Why is no one justified before God based on merit or good works? How then are we saved?

3. What reasons do people give for not working in the harvest? Are these valid? Why or why not?

4. Since you became a Christian, have you noticed a desire to tell others about what you have seen and heard and what you have experienced in your new life with Christ? Are you acting on that desire?

5. Do you know someone who needs the Lord? Begin praying for that person, and ask God to give you opportunities to share and testify of what Jesus has done in your life. When the opportunity arises (look for it!), boldly seize it. Get busy in the Father's harvest!

Lesson 7*
The "Ways" of Evangelism (Part 1)

Key Verse: *"But you shall receive power when the Holy Spirit has come upon you; and you shall be witnesses to Me in Jerusalem, and in all Judea and Samaria, and to the end of the earth"* (Acts 1:8 NKJV).

Key Scriptures:
1 John 1:3
1 Peter 3:15
John 4
Acts 1:8

Objective: The purpose of this lesson is to show from the Scriptures some of the ways to live out Christ's command to be a witness.

Introduction: Witnessing, or "winning," as we call it in the principle of twelve vision, is essential to our lives as Christians. Although the term *witnessing* conjures up all kinds of frightful thoughts in many people, it is actually something quite simple and applicable to all of us. To witness to someone simply means to tell what you have seen and heard. It's similar to being a witness in court. You do not have to prove anything, nor do you render the verdict; you simply take the stand and relate what you have seen and heard.

Christ calls His disciples to be faithful witnesses of what they have seen and heard of Him. As 1 John 1:3 NKJV so eloquently expresses: "That which we have seen and heard we declare to you." That is the only prerequisite

of a witness: to possess firsthand experience of something or someone. Then he relates, or witnesses, of what he has seen and heard.

I. Christians are called to be witnesses (Acts 1:8–11).

A. Jesus' last words issued the call to _____.

1. The last recorded words of Christ to His disciples before He ascended to heaven were that they would receive power from the Holy Ghost to become witnesses for Him.

2. Jesus' words are applicable to all who profess Him as Lord. They contain our marching orders until His return. This is our purpose, and this is our calling.

B. Jesus instructed the Gadarene demoniac to witness (Mark 5:1–20).

1. When Jesus delivered the Gadarene demoniac from the legion of demons, the man wanted to stay with Jesus (v. 18).

2. Jesus, however, would not allow this, but rather told him, "Go home to your family and tell them how much the Lord has done for you, and how he has had mercy on you" (v. 19 NIV).

3. After you get saved, it is natural to want to just stay with Jesus and enjoy His presence, but you must move past this and become a witness for Him.

C. Jesus called His disciples to be _____ of men (Matt. 4:19).

1. Early in His ministry, Jesus told His disciples that if they followed Him, He would make them into fishers of men. His purpose for them and His call to them was clear.

2. In saying this, Jesus revealed that the ultimate "catch" was to win a soul. This is what is accomplished through witnessing.

II. The Bible gives many examples of faithful witnesses.

A. The woman at the well in John 4 is an example of a witness.

1. The woman at the well experienced Jesus. She saw Him, touched Him, and received a word of knowledge from Him (vv. 17–18). The impact of what she saw and heard caused her to go and tell the people of her city what she had seen and heard. She was a witness.

2. The Bible says she "left her waterpot, went her way into the city, and said to the men, 'Come, see a Man who told me all things that I ever did. Could this be the Christ?' . . . And many of the Samaritans of that city believed in Him because of the word of the woman who testified, 'He told me all that I ever did' " (vv. 28–29, 39 NKJV).

B. Peter and John were faithful witnesses to the Resurrection.

1. Despite great opposition, Peter and John steadfastly proclaimed the Gospel. Nothing could deter them from speaking about what they knew to be true (Acts 4:1–20).

2. "So they called them and commanded them not to speak at all nor teach in the name of Jesus. But Peter and John answered and said to them, 'Whether it is right in the sight of

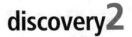
God to listen to you more than to God, you judge. For we cannot but speak the things which we have seen and heard' " (vv. 18–20 NKJV).

C. The apostle John was also a witness.

1. "That which was from the beginning, which we have heard, which we have seen with our eyes, which we have looked at and our hands have touched—this we proclaim concerning the Word of life. The life appeared; we have seen it and testify to it, and we proclaim to you the eternal life, which was with the Father and has appeared to us. We proclaim to you what we have seen and heard, so that you also may have fellowship with us" (1 John 1:1–3 NIV).

2. All that John proclaimed was from personal experience. He had seen Jesus and touched Him; now He was testifying of Him. He was a witness to the risen Christ, and no one could ever take that from him.

III. From the Bible, you can learn the ways of a witness.

A. A witness brings his _____ to Christ (John 1:40–42).

1. "Andrew, Simon Peter's brother, was one of the two who heard what John had said and who had followed Jesus. *The first thing Andrew did* was to find his brother Simon and tell him, 'We have found the Messiah' (that is, the Christ). And he brought him to Jesus" (John 1:40–42 NIV, emphasis added).

2. When something good happens to you, you immediately want to share the news with those closest to you. You can't wait to tell them about a raise at work or the

new car you bought. How much more should you desire to share Christ with them!

B.   A witness brings his _____ to Christ (John 1:45).

1.   Philip immediately told his friend Nathanael about Jesus. The Bible says he "found" Nathanael, thus indicating that he actively looked for him in order to share Jesus with him.

2.   You probably have a number of friends that do not know the Lord. Are you looking for opportunities to share Christ with them, or have you neglected the wonderful privilege of telling them what you know to be true?

C.   A witness gives testimony of Christ (Acts 26).

1.   Paul stood before King Agrippa and boldly testified of his faith in Christ. He was not intimidated by the king's position. He did not compromise his message, nor would he back down from it when challenged (vv. 24–25). He was a faithful witness.

2.   This had been Paul's pattern since his conversion: "Therefore, King Agrippa, I was not disobedient to the heavenly vision, but declared first to those in Damascus and in Jerusalem, and throughout all the region of Judea, and then to the Gentiles, that they should repent, turn to God, and do works befitting repentance" (vv. 19–20 NKJV).

D.   A witness is always _____ to give an answer for the hope within him (1 Pet. 3:15).

1. As a witness of Christ, you are on call 24/7 to share the Gospel. You must be ready at all times, always prepared to testify of Christ.

2. You must have a clear understanding of your hope in Christ and be able to clearly present this to others. Sometimes it is helpful to think through in advance what you would say if someone asked you to explain why you are a believer in Christ.

E. A witness is involved in the work of the harvest (Matt. 9:37).

1. Untold millions do not know Christ. Many are open and would respond to the Gospel if someone shared it with them. "The harvest is plentiful but the workers are few" (NIV).

2. You are called to be a laborer in the harvest fields of the world. It is not a responsibility that you can shirk. There is no one else to do it—only those who have already witnessed the reality of Christ.

F. A witness speaks from _____ experience (John 4).

1. As stated earlier, the woman at the well marveled that Jesus knew all about her, and she couldn't wait to share her experience with others (vv. 28–29).

2. You don't have to speak of what *others* have experienced; you only have to speak of what *you* have experienced. That makes you uniquely qualified to share the Gospel.

G. A witness preaches the Word (2 Tim 4:1–5).

1.   Never be afraid to preach the Word of God. Hide it in your heart, and be ready to bring it forth at any time.

2.   Peter in Acts 2 and Stephen in Acts 7 boldly proclaimed the Word of God in the power of the Holy Spirit. That's what witnesses do, and that's what you can do!

Summary: Jesus' last words are a powerful clue to His top priority: "You shall be witnesses." He has called us to be witnesses for Him until He returns. As witnesses, we tell others what we know about Jesus and what our experience has been. We don't have to prove the Gospel, and we don't have to have all the answers. All we really need is the courage and commitment to proclaim what Christ has done for us.

Questions and Discussion Points

1.   Do you consider yourself to be a faithful witness? Why or why not?

2.   What is your greatest hindrance to being an effective witness? What could you do to overcome it?

3.   Did someone witness to you of what God had done for him? What effect did his witness have on you?

4.   Have you committed yourself to obeying Jesus' command to be a witness to what you have seen and heard? If not, why not go ahead and do that now?

*Principles and ideas from this lesson were adapted from The Way of the Master by Kirk Cameron and Ray Comfort (Tyndale House Publishers, ©2004, Carol Stream, Illinois). For more information or to purchase related materials, visit www.wayofthemaster.com.

Lesson 8*
The "Ways" of Evangelism (Part 2)

Key Verse: *"Now we know that whatever the law says, it says to those who are under the law, so that every mouth may be silenced and the whole world held accountable to God. Therefore no one will be declared righteous in his sight by observing the law; rather, through the law we become conscious of sin"* (Rom. 3:19–20 NIV).

Key Scriptures:
Psalm 14:3; 19:7; 53:3
Proverbs 16:5; 20:6
Romans 2:15; 3:10, 12; 7:7
1 John 3:4
Galatians 3:11, 24

Objective: The purpose of this lesson is to identify biblical principles that directly affect the strategy, content, and goal of our evangelistic efforts.

Introduction: Jesus has finished His redemptive mission of suffering, dying on a cross, and being resurrected from the dead. The completion of Jesus' mission is the basis and the content of the good news of the Gospel. Jesus commissioned His followers (disciples) to take this Gospel to the ends of the earth to every tongue, tribe, and nation until He returns.

In this lesson, we want to recapture some biblical truths that many feel have been lost in this century's evangelistic efforts. The loss or ignorance of these truths has resulted in a dismal rate of retaining the fruit of many extensive and expensive evangelistic campaigns. That's because the church as a whole has lost sight of a basic truth from God that prepares a person to receive the Gospel. Without this biblical truth being employed, many persons respond to the Gospel for many unbiblical reasons, resulting in what some have termed "false conversions." On the other hand, using this truth as a tool can lead the lost to a true conversion that will last a lifetime.

I.   The _____ of God is the lost truth of biblical evangelism.

A.   The law converts the soul.

1.   Psalm 19 KJV says this in verse 7: "The law of the Lord is perfect, converting the soul."

2.   Because God's law is perfect, it has an inherent power within it to bring conversion.

B.   Many Christians do not understand the biblical purpose of the law in New Testament evangelism.

1.   They are afraid of the law, quoting Romans 6:15 that "we are not under law but under grace."

2.   Although that is true, it has also been used as an excuse to allow unbridled liberty in ways that were never meant.

II. God's law has several functions.

A. The law makes us _____ of our sin.

1. Romans 3:20 NIV says, "Therefore no one will be declared righteous in his sight by observing the law; rather, through the law we become conscious of sin."

2. In his groundbreaking message "Hell's Best Kept Secret," Ray Comfort notes that the word *conscious* refers to knowledge. Therefore, we see that the Bible teaches that it is the *law,* not our gospel presentations, that makes people conscious of their sin. Every person that would truly respond to the Gospel must *first* be conscious of his sin!

3. Romans 7:7 NIV says, "What shall we say, then? . . . Indeed I would not have known what sin was except through the law. For I would not have known what coveting really was if the law had not said, 'Do not covet.' "

B. The law confirms our _____ before God.

1. Romans 3:19 KJV says, "Now we know that what things soever the law saith, it saith to them who are under the law: that every mouth may be stopped, and *all the world may become guilty before God"* (emphasis added).

2. The law of God declares every person "guilty" before God. That is its basic purpose so that we might recognize our need for a savior.

C. The law _____ the tongues of the self-righteous.

1. Again in Romans 3:19 KJV, we see the phrase *that every mouth may be stopped* (silenced). When people try to justify themselves, the law stops them in their tracks, because no one has ever fully kept the law.

2. Proverbs 20:6 KJV says, "Most men will proclaim every one his own goodness." All people have a built-in tendency to see themselves as good. They judge themselves based upon their own standard of righteousness or the righteousness of others. When they or others are the standard by which they judge, more often than not, they come out okay.

3. However, God gave His law as the perfect standard by which all humanity will be judged. Since God is perfect (Matt. 5:48) and His law is perfect (Ps. 19:7), His standard for acceptable righteousness requires perfection. James 2:10 KJV says, "For whosoever shall keep the whole law, and yet offend in one point, he is guilty of all." So, even one sin renders us guilty.

4. When people are not aware of their sin and guilt before a holy God, they have a tendency to trust in their own righteousness and to justify themselves based on their own standards of self-righteousness. God gave the law, however, to show everyone that the standard of righteousness He requires is perfection.

5. When people realize that they will be judged by the law and that their self-righteousness falls short of God's perfect standard, they become conscious of their guilt and inability to save themselves. They then stop trying to justify themselves. Their tongues are silenced.

D.   The law is a _____ that brings us to Christ.

1. Galatians 3:24 KJV says "Wherefore the law was our schoolmaster *to bring us unto Christ,* that we might be justified by faith" (emphasis added). The Greek word for "schoolmaster" is *paedagogue* (from which we get our English word *pedagogue*). It refers to a slave who watched over the behavior of the young boys of the household. This slave was responsible for seeing that the boys got to the right place or person on time.

2. While the law cannot save us, it has a God-given purpose to show us that we need to be saved and thus leads us to Jesus as the answer.

III. The law has further truth in it.

A. **The biblical definition of sin is transgression of the law (1 John 3:4).**

B. **The law is good if it is used lawfully (1 Tim. 1:8).**

C. **The law was made for sinners (1 Tim. 1:9–10 NIV).**

1. This verse reads as follows: "We also know that law is made not for the righteous but for lawbreakers and rebels, the ungodly and sinful, the unholy and irreligious; for those who kill their fathers or mothers, for murderers, for adulterers and perverts, for slave traders and liars and perjurers—and for whatever else is contrary to the sound doctrine."

2. Since we are all sinners, the law applies to all of us. We are all lawbreakers.

IV. The law reveals the true state of humanity.

A. "All have _____ and fall short of the glory of God" (Rom. 3:23 NIV).

B. "There are none righteous, no, not one" (Rom. 3:10 KJV).

C. "Every one of them is gone back: they are altogether become filthy; there is none that doeth good, no, not one" (Ps. 53:3 KJV).

D. "And as it is appointed unto men once to die, but after this the judgment" (Heb. 9:27 KJV).

Summary: The law was given by God as a perfect standard to prick our consciences and make us aware of our sin. The law shows us that we are guilty of transgressing God's commands and deserving of His judgment. Because the law demands perfection, it silences our mouths from justifying ourselves based on our less than perfect righteousness. It then leads us to the quest for a savior who can make us righteous before a holy God. That quest ends when we find Jesus, the only one who ever kept the law perfectly.

Using the law of God as a witnessing tool leads people to first acknowledge their guilt before God. Then they can be receptive to their need for a savior. If we emphasize only what Jesus can do for us without explaining why we need Him, we shortchange people and set the stage for their conversion to be shallow at best and fleeting at worst.

Questions and Discussion Points

1. The apostle Paul in 2 Corinthians 13:5 NIV challenges the Corinthians: "Examine yourselves to see whether you are in the faith; test yourselves. Do you not realize that Christ Jesus is in you—unless, of course, you fail the test?" Have you ever examined, or tested, yourself to see whether you are truly in the faith? What kinds of questions should you ask yourself to determine the true condition of your soul?

2. How does the law lead us to Christ? What role did it play in your conversion?

3. Why are we sometimes reluctant to use the law as a witnessing tool? Why is it necessary?

4. Why is it not enough to proclaim the Gospel without sharing the law? How do the two work hand in hand?

*Principles and ideas from this lesson were adapted from *The Way of the Master* by Kirk Cameron and Ray Comfort (Tyndale House Publishers, ©2004, Carol Stream, Illinois). For more information or to purchase related materials, visit wayofthemaster.com.

Lesson 9*
The "How Tos" of Evangelism

Key Verse: *"But sanctify the Lord God in your hearts, and always be ready to give a defense to everyone who asks you a reason for the hope that is in you, with meekness and fear"* (1 Pet. 3:15 NKJV).

Key Scriptures:
Psalm 14:3; 19:7; 53:3
Proverbs 16:5; 20:6
Romans 2:15; 3:10, 12, 19–20; 7:7
1 John 3:4
Galatians 3:11, 24

Objective: The purpose of this lesson is to identify vital biblical principles that Jesus demonstrated when He witnessed to people during His time here on earth.

Introduction: When we consider the topic of evangelistic methods and content, we would do well to look closely and consider the One whom the Bible calls the "faithful witness" (Rev 1:5 NIV). Jesus is our example in everything, and that certainly applies to the area of sharing our faith. If we learn the methods Jesus used to share the Good News, then we can use those same methods when we witness to others.

Would you know what to say if someone came up to you and asked, "What must I do to be saved?" That's exactly what happened to Jesus, and from His example, we can learn how to answer that question, too.

I. The story of the rich young ruler illustrates several important aspects to sharing your faith (Matt. 19:16–22).

    A. Jesus first confronted man's _____ and self-righteousness (vv. 16–17 NIV).

        1. When the rich young ruler came to Jesus and asked what "good thing" he might do to gain eternal life, Jesus corrected him, saying, "Why do you ask me about what is good? . . . There is only One who is good" (v. 17). That One, of course, is God; no one else can lay claim to any inherent goodness.

        2. The Bible is very clear that no human being is good or righteous within himself: "There is none righteous, no, not one" (Rom. 3:10 NKJV). Good works, kind deeds, and nice thoughts do not make a person righteous.

        3. "God resists the proud but gives grace to the humble," says James 4:6 KJV. As long as a man is proud and trusts in his own goodness, he cannot appropriate the grace of God because he does not see his need for it. He must first be shown his lack of goodness before he is ready to receive the Gospel.

        4. Proverbs 20:6 KJV says, "Most men will proclaim every one his own goodness." Unregenerate people are full of pride and self-righteousness. They often compare themselves with others and conclude that at least they are not as bad as others they know. Their pride and self-righteousness must be dealt with before they can receive the Good News.

5.   Try this sometime: Go out in public and ask ten people you do not know, "Do you consider yourself to be a good person?" See if you get even one that says no!

     a.   Why is this true? If everyone is sinful and has fallen short of the glory of God, why do most people think they are good?

     b.   The answer is that they are using a standard other than the one God has provided to measure righteousness and goodness.

B.   **Jesus gave the law as the _____ for righteousness (Matt. 19:17b–19).**

1.   When the rich young ruler asked Jesus *what he had to do* to inherit eternal life, Jesus told him to keep the commandments of God (the law). He then listed five of the Ten Commandments and told the young man to keep them. Why did He do that? At first glance, it might seem like Jesus was advocating salvation by works rather than grace.

2.   Jesus pointed him to the law because He knew six things about the law and how it leads a person to recognize his need for salvation.

     a.   The law demands perfection and cannot be fully kept (James 2:10).

     b.   The law gives an awareness of sinfulness (Rom. 7:7).

     c.   The law quickens the _____ (Rom. 2:15).

     d.   The law reveals guilt before God (Rom. 3:19).

e.   Attempts to keep the law shatter false images of self-righteousness (Rom. 3:19).

f.   The law is a schoolmaster that leads us to Christ (Gal 3:23–24).

3.   The law is God's ordained tool to show a proud, self-righteous person that he is in need of a savior.

C.   Jesus kept coming back to the law (Matt. 19:20–21).

1.   Jesus did not tell sinners that they were sinners; He simply confronted them with the law. This is what He did with the rich young ruler. After Jesus listed several of the commandments, the young man countered with, "All these I have kept from my youth" (v. 20 NKJV). He continued in his self-righteousness and would not admit his own sin.

2.   The young man persisted in his self-righteous attitude, but Jesus continued to point him to the law. "Jesus said to him, 'If you want to be perfect, go, sell what you have and give to the poor, and you will have treasure in heaven; and come, follow Me' " (v. 21 NKJV). With this statement, Jesus summed up the entire law, which is to love God and to love your neighbor. The rich young ruler could not do this and was sad, thus for the first time recognizing his inability to keep the commands of God.

II.   There are several evangelism principles concerning the law that you can use in witnessing.

A.   Principle 1: "God opposes the _____" (James 4:6 NIV).

1. Jesus never presented the Good News to those who were proud and self-righteous. He refused to cast his pearls before swine (Matt. 7:6). You cannot get someone saved if he doesn't even know he is lost. That is the purpose of the law: to reveal a person's sinfulness and cause him to see his need for a savior.

2. If you follow Jesus' pattern, you might share the Gospel less, but you'll witness with the law more. As you witness with the law, the eyes of the lost are opened—perhaps for the first time—and they begin realizing that they are not as good as they thought they were. They begin seeing their need for someone to save them from their sins.

B. **Principle 2: God "gives grace to the humble" (James 4:6 NIV).**

1. Jesus spoke scathingly of those who were proud, puffed up, and self-righteous. When He spoke of the Pharisees and teachers of the law who thought that they were better than everyone else, He even used the terms *snakes* and *vipers* to describe them (Matt. 23:33). People like this are not ready to hear the Gospel because they think they have no need for it. They are blind to their own desperate spiritual condition.

2. Humility is required before a person can receive the Gospel. When someone is humble, God will move heaven and earth to extend saving grace to him. When Nicodemus, a Pharisee leader and teacher, came to Jesus with questions, Jesus took the time to talk to him and tell him exactly what salvation was all about (John 3:1–8). He looked into Nicodemus's heart and saw the humility that was prompting him to search for the truth. And Jesus responded.

C. **Principle 3: The law breaks the _____ heart.**

1. The law, not the Gospel, is God's ordained tool to break the hard heart and still the self-righteous tongue. Romans 3:19–20 NIV says, "Now we know that whatever the law says, it says to those who are under the law, so that every mouth may be silenced and the whole world held accountable to God. Therefore no one will be declared righteous in his sight by observing the law; rather, through the law we become conscious of sin."

2. The message of salvation from sin makes sense only after a person realizes he needs to be saved! If he responds to the Gospel for what he thinks he can gain from it (peace, love, fulfillment), without first seeing himself as a sinner in need of grace, he will likely not last long in his commitment to Christ.

D.   Principle 4: The _____ heals the broken heart with the good news of its message.

1. "The Lord is near to those who have a broken heart, and saves such as have a contrite spirit" (Ps. 34:18). The law "breaks"; the Gospel "heals." Used together, they have the power to lead every lost soul to Christ.

2. You might think that the law seems like a harsh taskmaster and find yourself somewhat reluctant to use it as a witnessing tool. However, many people have already found how truly effective it is, and you can experience that, too.

III.   Here's how to put into practice what you have learned about using the law as a witnessing tool.

A.   Go out in pairs.

    1.   Jesus sent His disciples out two by two (Luke 10:1), so when you go out to witness, go with someone else. You will feel more confident with a partner. You can encourage each other, and one can be praying while the other one is speaking.

    2.   On a more practical level, going out in pairs (especially for women) provides an added measure of physical safety.

B.   _____ the person you want to witness to.

    1.   Pray for the Holy Spirit to lead you to someone who is open, someone whose heart has already been prepared.

    2.   Then look for a person who is alone. Someone by himself will tend to be more honest and open than someone in a group. Peer influence occurs at all ages and levels of society, so avoid that added complication.

C.   Begin the conversation in a natural manner.

    1.   When Jesus ministered to the woman at the well, He began the conversation by asking for a drink of water (John 4:7). That was a very simple request, but it was the door that led to further interaction.

    2.   First Corinthians 2:14 says that the natural man does not understand the things of the Spirit; therefore, you must approach a person on a level that he can understand and

relate to. Comments on the weather, a local news event, an upcoming holiday, or a sports event are all things that you could use to start a conversation.

D.   Gradually move the conversation to the _____ realm.

1.   This is just what Jesus did with the woman at the well (John 4:10). He began with the natural but then related it to the spiritual. This is the point where many people falter in their witnessing.

2.   The Holy Spirit will help you. He will show you an opening and give you the courage to proceed. For example, suppose you approach someone and say, "Are you ready for Christmas?" (or any holiday). The two of you chat a while about your preparations for the holiday, and then you say, "You know, in church last Sunday my pastor had a really interesting insight about the holiday season." If the person seems agreeable, *briefly* share something that might interest him. Then you could say, "Where do you go to church?" Begin probing his spiritual background and follow that as far as you can.

3.   Another simple way to swing the conversation from the natural to the spiritual is to offer the person a tract and ask, "Do you have one of these?" When he takes it, simply say, "It's a gospel tract. Do you come from a Christian background?"

4.   Next, expose the person's self-righteousness by inquiring of his "goodness" (Prov. 20:6 NKJV). You might say, "Do you regard yourself as a good person?" If he says yes, ask him why he thinks he is good. Then ask, "Do you believe in the Ten Commandments?" Most will answer affirmatively.

5. Next, bring conviction, using the law of God. With the woman at the well, Jesus pointed out her adultery, the breaking of one of God's commandments (John 4:16–18). You might want to select several of the commandments and quiz the person about them. For example, you might say, "God's law says not to lie. Have you ever lied?" The person will probably answer yes. "What does that make you?" you counter with. "A liar," he responds. Do this with several commandments to show that he is a "lawbreaker."

6. By this point, the person will see that his perceived goodness before God is actually nonexistent. He will no longer be able to justify himself and hopefully will be ready to repent. Proceed with the conversation as far as the person will allow. If he is ready to get saved, great! Lead him in a prayer for salvation and begin immediately to connect him to a church. If he does not want to pray, that's okay, too. You will have planted a seed that will germinate at a later time.

7. Always end the witnessing on a positive note. Always be respectful and courteous, and do not get involved in debating or arguing. Remember: You represent Christ!

Summary: God gave the law as a perfect standard to ignite out consciences and make us aware of our sin. The law shows us that we are guilty of transgressing God's commands and are deserving of His judgment. Because the law demands perfection, it silences our mouths from justifying ourselves based on our less than perfect righteousness. The law is a taskmaster that is designed to lead us to Christ. It is a powerful, effective tool that we can use when witnessing to others.

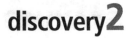
Questions and Discussion Points

1. What are some things that people base their perception of "goodness" on? Why are these inadequate?

2. Have you ever led anyone to Christ? If so, what was it like? Did it make you want to witness all the more? If not, would you like to be used in this way? (Answer honestly!) Begin praying and asking the Lord to give you both the desire and the opportunity to be a witness for Him (Col. 4:2–6).

3. Get together with one other person in the class and take turns practicing using the law as a witnessing tool.

4. Before next week's class, ask three people you do not know if they consider themselves to be good people. If God gives opportunity, practice the witnessing tools shared in this lesson.

*Principles and ideas from this lesson were adapted from *The Way of the Master* by Kirk Cameron and Ray Comfort (Tyndale House Publishers, ©2004, Carol Stream, Illinois). For more information or to purchase related materials, visit www.wayofthemaster.com.

Lesson 10
Understanding the Needs of New Believers

Key Verse: *"But we were gentle among you, just as a nursing mother cherishes her own children. . . . as you know how we exhorted, and comforted, and charged every one of you, as a father does his own children"* (1 Thess. 2:7, 11 NKJV).

Key Scriptures:
1 Peter 2:2; 5:8
Hebrews 6:1–3; 10:39
1 John 2:15–17; 4:7; 5:13
Galatians 5:16–17, 24–25
Ephesians 1:6
Acts 2:46–47; 9:1–9, 17–20; 11:23; 20:20
2 Peter 1:4
2 Corinthians 1:20
Psalm 1:1–3
John 4:23–24; 5:8, 9, 14; 10:27
Philippians 4:6, 19

Objective: In this lesson, the student will explore the basic requirements for continued spiritual growth in the lives of new believers.

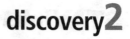

Introduction: Just as a plant needs the right conditions and environment for growth, new believers also need certain basic things if they are going to be able to grow and flourish in their new lives in Christ. If these basic needs are not met, they will struggle along in their newfound faith or actually even die.

When a child is born, he does not automatically thrive. If not lovingly cared for, he will die. He is totally dependent upon others for the first few years of his life. When people are born again and become children in God's family, they, too, need care and concern. Our role as more mature Christians is to show them the love and attention they need to become firmly rooted in Christ.

I.   New believers need _____.

A.   The devil is an adversary who is looking to destroy them (1 Pet. 5:8).

1.   In the animal kingdom, the young, the old, and the weak are prime prey for their enemies. Because they are defenseless, they are easy targets. It's the same way in the kingdom of God. New believers are easy targets for the devil's schemes and attacks.

2.   One of the most important ministries that the church can provide to new believers is a covering of prayer and intercession. Paul constantly was in prayer for the new churches and new believers that had come to know the Lord (Eph. 1:15–16; 1 Thess. 1:2–3).

3.   The greatest means of providing protection to new believers is to intercede for them in the same way that Jesus intercedes for us (Heb. 7:25).

B.   **The world constantly tries to draw new believers back to itself (Heb. 10:39; 1 John 2:15–17).**

    1.   Jesus said in Mark 4:18–19 that the cares and worries of the world will choke out God's Word and keep new believers from developing fruit.

    2.   It is absolutely essential, therefore, that new believers receive the solid teaching of the Word of God to help them become rooted and grounded in the Lord (Col. 2:6–7). Only then will they be able to resist the temptations of the world.

    3.   It is the responsibility of the more mature Christians to teach new believers how to use the Word of God as a tool to hold them steady against the pull of the world.

C.   **The _____ naturally desires to regain control (Gal. 5:16–17, 24–25).**

    1.   The term *the flesh* refers to the old way of living apart from the lordship of Jesus Christ. Old ways and habits don't easily die, even after a person becomes born again. The flesh will always resist what the Holy Spirit wants.

    2.   New believers need encouragement and exhortation on how to walk in the leading of the Holy Spirit. Through the example of other believers who have already learned this, they learn how to subdue the flesh (1 Cor. 4:16–17).

II.   New believers need to be _____.

A.   **They need the assurance of their salvation (1 John 5:13).**

1. One of the most used weapons in the arsenal of the enemy is doubt and unbelief. New believers, therefore, must learn to base their faith on more than feelings, because feelings eventually fade. New believers need to know that their salvation is based on the surety of God's Word, not on circumstances, trials, or emotions.

2. Always point new believers to the Word of God concerning the promise of the gift of eternal life (John 8:31–32; 10:10).

3. They need to know how much God loves them and cares for them. They need to experience His great love for them and to grab hold of the promises that He has given them.

B. They need the acceptance of the _____ (Eph. 1:6 NKJV; 1 John 4:7).

1. All newborns need the love and care of parents. Love and acceptance are the primary factors in the development of healthy and well-balanced children, both naturally and spiritually.

2. New believers need the fellowship of strong believers (Acts 2:46–47).

3. Jesus said that one of the hallmarks of His followers would be the love they showed for one another (John 13:35).

C. They need new friends (Acts 9:17–20).

1.   Immediately following the conversion of Saul (Paul), God sent him a new friend and mentor, Ananias.

2.   Ananias greeted Paul as a brother, prayed for him, led him into water baptism, prayed for him to be filled with the Holy Spirit, and introduced him to the believers in Damascus.

3.   All new believers need a close network of believers that will befriend them and share the comfort and encouragement of God the Father with them (2 Cor. 1:4).

III.   New believers need to be fed the Word of God.

A.   They need God's milk (1 Pet. 2:2).

1.   Every child needs milk to grow. New believers need the simple truths of the Word of God to encourage and strengthen them.

2.   The Word of God is the most basic, essential nourishment for new believers. Without it, they will die spiritually; with it, they will grow and mature into faithful disciples of the Lord.

B.   They need God's _____ (2 Pet. 1:4; 2 Cor. 1:20).

1.   New believers need to discover all that God has promised them. Faith must be established upon what God has promised He would do for those who trust Him.

2. As new believers discover the truth of God's promises, their faith will grow by leaps and bounds. Their faith will become personal, meaningful, and applicable to daily life.

C.   They need God's _____ (Acts 20:20; Heb. 6:1–3; Ps. 1:1–3).

1. New believers need to know the counsel of God for their lives and the sound, clear, and life-giving teachings of the Word of God.

2. New believers need to learn how to avoid the counsel of the ungodly and how to meditate on the Word of God. This will bring them blessing and success.

IV.   New believers need _____ with God.

A.   They need to learn how to worship God (John 4:23–24).

1. God is looking for worshipers, those who have surrendered to Him and given Him control over their lives.

2. Worshipers look to God to give them living water that causes them to never thirst again. God is the source of living water to those who worship and adore Him, and new believers must learn this.

B.   They need to know how to talk to God (Phil. 4:6, 19).

1.   God wants His children to bring every need to Him. He wants them to talk to Him about the things that burden them. This is one of the vital aspects of prayer and something that new believers must learn to do.

2.   When we keep our hearts free from worry, we can make our requests known to God, knowing He will meet every one of them according to His riches and glory. As new believers learn this truth, their faith in a loving Father who hears their prayers begins to grow.

C.   They need to learn how to hear God's voice (John 10:27).

1.   Jesus promised to speak to His sheep, that is, His followers. New believers must learn how to develop a listening ear to the voice of the Lord. They do not automatically know how to do this, but they will grow in their ability to recognize His voice if more mature Christians help them.

2.   Jesus promised that He would sit down and fellowship with those who hear His voice and respond to it (Rev. 3:20).

V.   New believers need _____.

A.   They need immediate follow-up (John 5:1–9, 14).

1.   After healing a man who had been lame for thirty-eight years, Jesus wasted no time in encouraging and exhorting him. He provided direction and instruction for the man so that he could maintain the healing he had received.

2. New believers need someone to immediately follow up on them after they get saved. In this way, their salvation can be affirmed, and they can immediately begin the lifelong process of becoming a follower of Jesus.

B.   They need consistent _____ (Acts 11:23).

1. Barnabas found a group of new believers that had just received salvation. He exhorted and encouraged them to keep moving forward and going deeper in Christ.

2. Barnabas's name means "son of encouragement." Many times in the New Testament, this facet of his character is mentioned. In the same way, new believers in the church need someone who will care enough to take time with them and encourage them in their new commitment to Christ.

C.   They need to be a part of a life-giving cell group (Acts 2:46–47).

1. The believers spent time together and shared meals. New believers need to be in cells where there is the sharing of love and life.

2. A life-giving cell is one in which new believers feel welcomed and at home. A life-giving cell is one in which people are coming to know Jesus and are growing in their faith in Christ.

D.   They need an _____ with God (Acts 9:1–9).

1. Paul had an encounter with God that totally and radically changed his life. All new believers need an encounter with God that will bring total life transformation.

2.   Paul's encounter brought him a new vision. Similarly, new believers need to discover the purpose that God has for them.

3.   New believers need the healing and delivering work of the Holy Spirit. At a three-day Encounter Retreat, new believers have the opportunity to experience the ministry and infilling of the Holy Spirit, the healing power of the cross, and the power of God to become all that God has destined them to be.

Summary: New believers need the love and care of older, more mature Christians in the body of Christ. When they first enter the kingdom of God, new believers are innocent, vulnerable, and fragile, just like newborn babies. But as they receive the attention they need, they grow and blossom into strong, stable believers full of faith and endurance.

We who have followed Christ for a greater length of time owe it to new believers to take them under our wings and guide them in their Christian journey and discovery of faith. We need to protect them, love them, accept them, and spiritually feed them. We need to teach them how to commune with God, and we need to see that they receive the ministry they need. In short, we need to do for them what others have done for us.

Questions and Discussion Points

1.   From what three things do new believers need protection?

2.   What happens to new believers who base their salvation on feelings? What should be the basis of their faith? What role, if any, do emotions play in the life of faith?

3.   How does knowing God's promises in His Word build faith in new believers?

4.   Discuss the role of the cell group in meeting the needs of new believers. How did being part of a cell help you in your early days of being a Christian?

5.   What does the Encounter Retreat do for new believers? Why is it so important to their spiritual development?

Continuing the Discovery . . .

Congratulations! You've achieved another milestone in your discovery of who you are in Christ. You've learned about the vision God has for the world and the important part you play in seeing it come to pass. You've learned all about praise and worship and spiritual warfare. You've learned how to get a vision from God and then use it in His kingdom. You've charted your vision and are beginning to conquer your land. Your life with Christ has become a wonderful adventure of discovery and purpose.

Are you ready for the next step in your Christian walk? Then get ready for Discovery 3—the next level in your Christian training! We'll emphasize leadership development and skills, and you'll soon be in a position to multiply yourself in your own team of twelve. You'll continue growing and learning and experience the thrill of forming a team of power-filled believers to work alongside you.

You have proven that you can *stay the course,* so we hope you'll continue with us and *reach the summit* in your wonderful discovery of Christ!

Answer Key

Charting Your Vision

Lesson 1

Page 12
Values

Page 13
Serving
Brokenness

Page 14
Harvest

Page 15
Serving

Lesson 2

Page 20
Relationship
Pastor

Page 22
Connected

Lesson 3

Page 28
Order

Page 29
Excellence

Page 30
Obedience

Page 31
Authority
Holiness

Lesson 4

Page 38
Conquest

Page 39
Boldness
Warriors

Page 40
Courage
Consecration

Page 41
Commitment

Page 42
Conquest

Lesson 5

Page 48
Seeing
Walking

Page 49
Training

Page 50
Giving
Believing

Lesson 6

Page 56
Church

Page 57
Leadership
Pastoring

Page 58
Grows
Strengthens

Page 59
Gifts

Page 60
Relationships,
activity
Accountability

Lesson 7

Page 66
Multiplication
Connecting

Page 67
Supplication

Page 68
Sanctification

Page 69
Schedule

Page 70
Selection

Lesson 8

Page 76
Urgency

Page 77
Goals

Page 78
Assess
Evaluate

Page 80
Power of the Lord

Lesson 9

Page 86
Mission
Fruitfulness

Page 87
Vision

Page 88
Fear,
discouragement
Passivity

Page 89
Carnality
Word of God

Page 90
Holy Spirit
Cross

Page 91
Prayer
Obedience

Page 92
Unity

Lesson 10

Page 98
Greatness

Page 99
Measure

Page 100
Ointment

Page 101
Servant's

Page 102
Master
Deny

Page 103
Faithful
Humble

Conquering Your Land

Lesson 1

Page 112
Praise
Honoring

Page 113
Blessing
Sacrifice
Weapon

Page 114
Worship

Page 116
Spirit
Heart
Will

Page 117
Words
Sing

Page 118
Entire life

Lesson 2

Page 122
God
Darkness

Page 123
Lies
Accuser

Page 124
Mind

Page 125
Word of God

Page 126
Recognize
Reject
Resist
Truth

Page 127
Faith

Page 128
Name of Jesus
Testimony

Lesson 3

Page 132
Abraham

Page 133
Moses

Page 134
Intercessor

Page 135
Priesthood
Channel
Praise

Page 136
Faith
Wait

Lesson 4

Page 141
Souls
Prayer of three

Page 142
Fast
Scripture
Needs

Lesson 5

Page 146
Cost

Page 148
Snare
No one

Page 149
Blinded
Price

Lesson 6

Page 154
Lost

Page 155
Sinners

Page 156
Seek, save
Life

Page 157
Dead

Page 158
Condemned

Page 159
Multitudes,
multitudes

Page 160
Go
Preach
Repentance
Send
Witnesses

Lesson 7

Page 164
Witness
Fishers

Page 166
Family

Page 167
Friends
Ready

Page 168
Personal

Lesson 8

Page 172
Law

Page 173
Conscious
Guilt
Silences

Page 174
Schoolmaster

Page 176
Sinned

Lesson 9

Page 180
Pride

Page 181
Standard
Conscience

Page 182
Proud

Page 183
Hard

Page 184
Gospel

Page 185
Select

Page 186
Spiritual

Lesson 10

Page 190
Protection

Page 191
Flesh
Loved

Page 192
Church

Page 193
Promises

Page 194
Counsel
Communion

Page 195
Ministry

Page 196
Encouragement
Encounter

BOOKS IN THIS SERIES

The Journey to Freedom: An Encounter With God
The Journey is a three-step process that takes new believers *to the cross* (four-week course), *through the cross* (Encounter Retreat), and then teaches them how to walk *with the cross* (seven-week course).

Discovery 1: Finding the Rock
The Discovery classes immediately follow the completion of the Journey. In this first book, the focus is on building a firm foundation in Christ and strengthening the family.

Discovery 2: Staying the Course
The second Discovery book launches the student into a lifestyle of vision and conquest in the principle of twelve. He learns how to chart his vision and conquer his land for Christ.

Discovery 3: Reaching the Summit
In this final book of the Discovery series, the student develops solid principles of leadership for a lifetime of fruitfulness. He learns all about the power and ministry of a team of twelve and the role of the Holy Spirit in making him a leader of leaders.

To order, or for more information, visit bethany.com or bccn.com.
Or, call 225-771-1600.